ROYAL AMERICAN INJUSTICE II

BLATANT RACISM—DELIBERATE MURDER

DAVID QUINTON BROOKS

PAGE PUBLISHING
Conneaut Lake, PA

First originally published by Page Publishing 2024

ISBN 979-8-88654-452-7 (pbk)
ISBN 979-8-88654-455-8 (digital)

Printed in the United States of America

This book is dedicated solely for my Grandfather

A young pic of Royal Cyril Brooks

GRETNA COP KILLS BUS RIDER

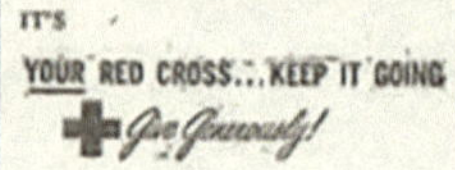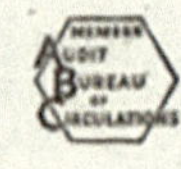

Vol. XXIII. No. 24 — NEW ORLEANS 13, LA., SATURDAY, MARCH 6, 1948

Witnesses Feel Fatal Shooting Unwarranted

Flying shots from the frenzied gun of Patrolman Alvin Bladsacker of the Gretna police force snuffed out the life of Roy Cyril Brooks, Jr., 44, 616 Fried Street, Gretna, La., at about 5:15 last Friday evening, Feb. 27.

Brooks, two shots in his stomach, died in the shadow of the Jefferson Parish Courthouse on Huey P. Long Avenue.

Bladsacker alleges Brooks struck him twice following his arrest on a Westwego bus at the Gretna ferry landing. He shot Brooks, he said, because it was the only means whereby he could bring the "resisting" man under control.

According to persons on the scene, Brooks was under the influence of drink and was unaware of his behavior. Many Negroes and whites feel that the fatal shooting could have been avoided.

Bladsacker, who was on duty directing traffic at the ferry landing, alleges that Brooks boarded the Westwego bus, drunk and abusive, refused to pay his fare. He said that he was called to quiet Brooks and, failing to do so, ordered him to leave the bus.

Brooks, Bladsacker stated, hit him in the jaw, almost knocking him from the bus. He then got Brooks off the bus and was marching him on Huey P. Long Avenue to the jail three blocks away when Brooks hit him on the head, making a motion, Bladsacker alleges, as if to draw a weapon.

"Frightened," Bladsacker pulled out his revolver and fired two shots which struck Brooks in the stomach.

Brooks was pronounced dead at about 5:55 p. m. by Dr. Charles Gethinx Jefferson Parish coroner.

Brooks is survived by his wife, Mrs. Mary Brooks, and two sons, Roy C. Brooks Jr., 11, veteran of the 92d and 1½ years service in the army, and Pfc. Herman Lawrence Brooks, 18, presently in the U. S. Army at Smoky Hill Airfield, Celina, Kan., and a daughter.

PTA Groups Endorse Public School Program

By the end of next week most of the Parent-Teacher organizations of the 36-odd public schools...

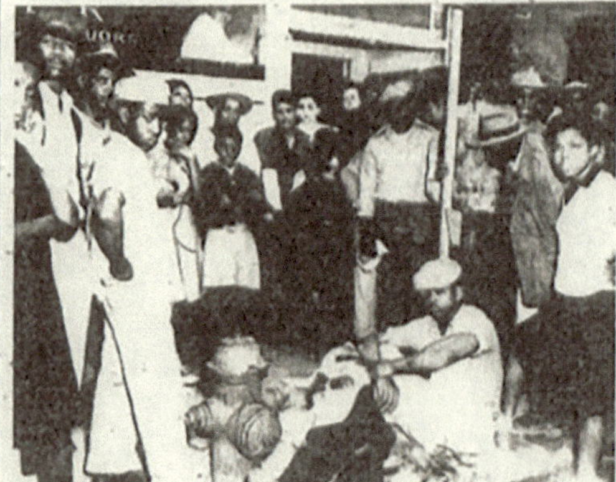

Slain By Gretna Policeman

A crowd of curious onlookers view the body of Roy C. Brooks, Sr., who was fatally wounded by Patrolman Alvin Bladsacker of the Gretna police force. His death was believed to have been the result of the frenzied attempts of Bladsacker to arrest him on a disorderly conduct charge. The policeman firing two shots into the slain man's stomach at close range. Roy Brooks Jr., son of the slain man, sits near his father's prostrate body.—(Photo by Port.)—EXCLUSIVE WEEKLY PHOTO!

10,000 Members Is Goal Of NAACP's '48 Drive; Marshall Speaker Mar. 14

Setting the New Orleans Branch NAACP's goal at 10,000 members, Paul A. Landin, 1948 campaign chairman, said Saturday that...

BLAZE OUT SAFE CRACKING

Unknown Assailants Make Escape

Blazing revolvers, roaring in the March winds, snuffed out the lives of two youths in Negro communities Monday and Tuesday of this week. (Negro policemen in the solution in giving law-abiding citizens adequate police protection.) Local police still seek unidentified assailants of the two men.

In the initial incident, early Monday morning, Ernest Bean, 4417 Baudin Street, fell under eight shots fired at him from a .45 caliber automatic near bullet striking him in the neck and two others entering his back.

According to persons present, Bean and a companion came involved in an argument at a bar at 8000 Eagle Street about midnight Sunday. Following the argument and leaving the bar, Bean and his companion...

2nd Vote Denial

Roy Brooks (Uncle Papi) A WWII Veteran who never
saw justice for his father Royal Cyril Brooks.
Photo provided by Weekly Advocate Louisiana.

CHAPTER 1

Wrongful Killing

This story requires a second book so that I, David Quinton Brooks, the fifth and the youngest son of Herman Lawrence Brooks, and my father, Royal Cyril Brooks, youngest child—which makes me the youngest grandchild—of Royal Cyril Brooks, might bring awareness to all Americans and the world of the willfully hidden story of the injustice done to my grandfather, Royal Cyril Brooks, on February 27, 1948, 3:00 in the afternoon, in the city of Gretna, Louisiana, where he lost his life due to violent police brutality, racial injustice, and a judicial system that was—and is—clearly racist toward the Black race. A system that has been racist from the founding of this country.

Due to the racism and suppression and Black rights being violated, White law enforcement and White civilians could do anything they pleased to a Black American citizen, including horrific lynchings, beatings, and murder. White law enforcement and White citizens would rarely be held accountable for their crimes and atrocities during the Jim Crow era.

So my grandfather, Royal Cyril Brooks, a United States of America civil rights martyr, has been overlooked. His story has been concealed for more than seventy years until it was researched by Northeastern University School of Law—Center, Boston, Massachusetts, under the Civil Rights and Restorative Justice Project. when it comes to the death of Royal Cyril Brooks, it was a cruel act of White supremacy in the deep south, and White-run racist law enforcement would not be held accountable or face punishment for the crime that was committed against my grandfather, which was a cowardly act, done by a so-called honest peace officer who murdered my grandfather in cold blood and in broad daylight, in front of hundreds of eyewitnesses. Yet all types of excuses were made, and lies were told to protect a police officer, who clearly committed an unprovoked murder.

We must ask ourselves, where is the accountability in a so-called civilized country, when anyone that is unarmed and defenseless can be shot in the back and then shot in the side, at point-blank range by a law enforcement officer—which was exactly how my grandfather was murdered by a racist, White city of Gretna, Louisiana, traffic police officer? It raises some fundamental questions about how your law enforcement officer escaped punishment!

Obviously, if you are shot in the back by a lethal, police-issued .38 revolver while the officer is walking you to the local jail, and you never saw it coming, the action committed by a law enforcement officer would be certain death due to his training. Apparently, my grandfather was not resisting his arrest, only questioning it, for a disagreement over a five-cent bus fare, so was it necessary for him to shoot Royal Cyril Brooks? And then the police officer proceeded to shoot him a second time! I call that a hate crime by a person who clearly resents Black people.

The law was broken right then and there. You do not shoot a human being in the back, when they are totally at your mercy—which is wrong—and you, as a law enforcement officer, have a decision to make, which is right or wrong, and the choice that was made was the wrong one—to take a human life for such a harmless interaction.

So America needs to take a closer look at its practices, which have been against the Black man for centuries. They are responsible for the loss of many innocent Black lives. Millions of Black human beings have been terminated because of White supremacy over many centuries because of their hate and resentment toward the Black race.

So will America admit to being guilty of crimes against Black humanity? Will the city of Gretna, Louisiana, police department publicly admit that the senseless act committed by one of their so-called heroic law enforcement officer was a premeditated murder instead of saying, "We cannot comment on what happened seventy years ago"? But Royal Cyril Brooks' grandchildren are waiting for you to be accountable.

The killing of Royal Cyril Brooks was a racially motivated murder! And will they come forward and admit that it was a kangaroo court that acquitted the traffic police officer of first-degree premeditated homicide? Because that is how I see it, and the majority of Blacks in America feel the same way.

With an all-White, all-male jury in 1948—which we already know proves that they are racist—in the deep south, in a former Confederate southern state, with a very racist White government in Louisiana, an innocent Black man would never receive a fair and equal trial. My grandfather did not commit a crime; he was on his way to work. But Royal Cyril Brooks became a victim of violent police brutality, deliberate murder, and blatant racism.

That is not justice. The police officer got away with a racially motivated murder, being protected by a racist government. Homicide is murder at the hands of another human being. His death was not an accident, suicide, or undetermined. He was shot at point-blank range in the back and in his side, defenseless and unarmed, with both hands raised in the air while clutching a bag of peanuts. So I guess that they consider a bag of peanuts a deadly weapon. So his life was taken over a five-cent bus fare, but they called it a justifiable homicide.

You want us to forget the violent nature that you subjected my grandfather, Royal Cyril Brooks, to with your twisted ways. It would be absurd. The trauma has been passed down for generations, and the Brooks are still affected to this day.

So the same thing is this: Black people have generations of poverty, racism, injustice, and economic disparity, while Whites have generations of prosperity, wealth, justice, and economic superiority over everyone in this country, and continue to get rich off of the modern-day slave labor, off of the Black race to this very day.

Many corporations and major banks today have participated in slavery by owning and selling slaves and made a fortune off us, yet they are silent because they know for a fact that they owe the true descendants of slaves an apology and a great sum of—to put it plainly—money because forced labor, but they refuse to pay up. All of you must be—and you will be—held accountable. Your hands are stained with blood.

When you hear the truth being spoken, some way you try to silence it or try to claim it is a lie being told because whoever exposes you, you try to deny it.

You refuse to accept the fact that your past ways are so horrific that you'll go as far as to say, "That was the past. We don't have anything to do with that." But you do. You are benefiting from the wealth that was gained from slavery, attained by forced free labor, and you refuse to pay the descendants of slaves that you owe to this day. So you can't wipe away the sins of your descendants and their violent, hateful, and racist behavior because the traits have been genetically passed down to you. The same type of attitude is present to this very day; only most of you have been clever enough not to let your true feelings out. If you need a reminder, look at the news, television, radio, and social media—racism and injustice are running rampant!

Now it is a fight against good and evil, which it always has been. Their race is so sick that the crimes that they have committed against Blacks in America would shame them to embarrassment and humiliation to the end of time. But they are determined to try to project an image that they are the cleanest and fairest of individuals, with morals and compassion, which is false.

If you do not believe what I am saying, this part of their so-called history will say otherwise, and answer all questions of doubt. Look at their movies that have been produced from the 1930s to now! They have told on themselves. Look how they show you how greedy, diabolical, and dangerous they are—breaking the law and killing to get ahead, even against their own race, and the way they treat the Black race with total domination as well as other races of color to show their superiority. So you better believe that those Jim Crow films will not be boycotted or destroyed because they call it history.

So they are the ones who created the crime in this country. We were not able to commit any crime, because being a slave, you would basically be putting your life on the line if you stole something, or rebelled against them, and so it is impossible for us to have any type of criminal history in the infancy of the United States of America when they were in total control of the country. And they still have total control to this very day. So we know who invented crime in America. But somehow, we are the victims of their own creation, from the suppression of equality to their blatant racism right in our faces, and we are too blind to see it, at least the masses. So we all must bring up the question, What is next? What can be done? What will be done? All I hear is certain so-called celebrities, in politics, sports, and entertainment talk about change, and nothing is getting done.

The only reason that their voices are being heard is that they have a little money, and so no matter how much they say they care about the Black citizens in the United States, at the end of the day, they will go home to their luxurious homes in the suburbs without a worry in the world, while the same conditions exist in every inner-city and ruined town in America.

What makes them better than the average individual? Absolutely nothing! As I stated before in my first book, everyone is equal; no one is greater than the next person. They are no smarter than your next-door neighbor, and in many instances, the average neighbor is far more intelligent, but their voices will never be heard.

So as you can read, the preferential treatment is given when you have money, so how dare they speak about what we must deal with on a daily, especially when you watch the events unfold on television from the comfort of your suburban homes, miles away from the madness, and you so-called celebrities are not my voice. And millions of others feel the same way. You are speaking from outside of the bubble looking in, and your so-called celebrity status has no influence on how the government is being run. All it is, is fake talk, and nothing is truly getting accomplished!

Until racism, inequality, and major economic injustice for the millions of Blacks—who are living in poverty, off of a peasant's income—are seriously addressed in this country, there will be the same old protesting and marching, police brutality, and rioting, and it will get worse. And what is sad is that the young kids and teenagers are watching all of this turmoil occurring right before their eyes. So just think of the devastating effect it is going to have on their lives when they grow up.

My grandfather, Royal Cyril Brooks, was subjected to the same type of racism as today but just at a different time in history, not too long ago, in 1948.

His story has been willfully hidden and overlooked. That bothers me, but that is about to change because I refuse to be silent about his injustice. America must be told of the murder of Royal Cyril Brooks, slain by a racist White city of Gretna, Louisiana traffic police officer, a major tragedy in America, swept under the rug to hide their malice and resentment toward Black people. The sick history that they have on their resume cannot be removed; it will follow them to the end, and that is when they will receive their punishment from the Almighty God for the cruel and brutal treatment of his Native Black American people, who are a new race of Black people in North America, descendants of slaves, who are subjected to their command as though they are God.

White supremacists in this country and in the world have been hiding the true history and distorting the truth of the world for an extremely long time. They reverse the truth, they take God's words from the Bible and add their own words, which is a sin against *the Almighty God*! And all of you White supremacists will be judged accordingly when your life is over on earth.

If you need facts about what I am saying, all of the research has been done by Dr. Claud Anderson, who has done extensive research concerning the deliberate destruction of the Black race.

So, if you are not a God-fearing individual, I feel sorry for you, because the punishment of the Almighty God is something to fear.

Now this problem with emancipation means one thing that a lot of Black people do not know, or refuse to acknowledge: It is the creation of the new slave, making a new slave for the future.

So take a close look at what is going on in this country. You have reverse slavery in the United States of America.

First, we are in chains for over four hundred years. Now with mass incarceration today, Black men are back in chains due to their invention called crime, held in their creation called a cell, and warehoused just like back in slavery like an animal, under lock and key for twenty-four hours a day, 365 days a year; disrespected and humiliated as a human being and fed slop that a dog would not eat; deprived of the other sex, family, and your children; and secluded from society, only to die alone and miserable, the same way a slave would live and die. And you better believe they will spend tens of millions of dollars to keep you incarcerated.

So slavery never left us. We were never freed; we were made new—a new slave. Wake up, Black America! Do not be fooled anymore.

So here we go with more deception from our slave masters, who continue to trick Black America to this day. To keep us in the crab barrel, they have chosen handpicked Black people who do not mind eating leftovers from their master's plates, and they will do whatever it takes to please and protect them.

Honestly, do you think we are supposed to be content with you making more interracial television shows? But many will fall for your deception, putting us on more TV commercials, to project an image to the world that everything is okay, just honky dory, which is part of your plot to keep our minds off of the factual issues. And you know that many Black people will fall for your trick in order to gain wealth and fame! And the roles that they give a Black man in their commercials, television shows, and movies are just degrading.

So in reality, it is one big powder keg waiting to erupt into a race war, and that is what you want so you can exterminate a massive amount of the Black race. You have control of all of the weapons and resources. You say that about 23 percent of Black Americans are in poverty. But I do not believe your count because I have been to all forty-eight connected states, and from the disparity I have seen, I know it is higher. So how can we protect ourselves? We are at your mercy because you have been making manufactured diseases, poisoning food and water for tens of decades only for it to backfire, killing your own race.

But finally, with the help of foreigners, you have succeeded in creating COVID-19 and it is airborne and it is killing Black people in a certain age group at an alarming rate. That's why Republicans and Democrats refuse to take care of the Black people in this country because their plan is working and it's killing Black people. And you better believe that both political parties are working hand-in-hand, together keeping the Black race in this country confused and tricked.

See, man cannot make peace in society without the help, guidance, and power of the Almighty God. Man refuses to seek the help of our Lord and Savior, Jesus Christ, so the end result will be the destruction of humankind as we know it.

So the ones that are in control of the earth all need to beg for forgiveness—before it is too late for them—from the ALMIGHTY GOD, and with his word and direction, we can defeat racism and economic injustice, which is a disease to every living Black human being on earth.

The United States government is reluctant to address the problems in society. They would like the same old ways to continue and to distract us from the key issues concerning this country.

We, as a Black race of people, need to focus on trying to better ourselves, instead of concentrating on worldly possessions. That's part of the distraction.

Since the 1960s and even before, we have been crying for equal rights, and now in 2020, they claim that they are dedicated to improving and reforming the practices of the government, and law enforcement. So in other words, civil rights activists wasted their time sixty years ago, and many years before—things are worse now than in the past. So it took them over half a century to realize that change is needed in American law—after the killings of Black Americans were getting out of control—when change was needed centuries ago.

The secret agenda must come to a halt, and the domination of Black people must come to an end. We have been fighting for the same cause well before I was born and well before my father and grandfather were given the divine right to live on earth by the Almighty and Heavenly Father God, only for Royal Cyril Brooks to have his life taken away by some distorted, racist White supremacist police officer, who now regrets his action because he is deceased, along with my grandfather, and he has no other choice but to face him, Royal Cyril Brooks, and his children—Herman L Brooks, my father; Roy Brooks Jr., my uncle; and Bertha Mike (Brooks), my aunt—with the Almighty Father God present.

The father of lies has deceived the White race with an abundance of false promises and trickery, and when it is all over, they'll see that they have been condemned to the lake of fire for all of the crimes committed against humankind. It does not take fancy words to get the facts out; simply basic knowledge for the masses to understand.

You would be surprised to know just how many people of all races have sold their souls just for money, worldly possessions, and fame, only to be sentenced to damnation for falling prey to evil deception.

What I do not understand is that the human race is really confused. Everyone is exactly the same, yet for some strange reason, having a different skin color determines how your life on earth will be lived. If you have any type of light to dark-brown complexion, you can expect to be met with all types of obstacles and racism. But if you are White, you will be granted all types of rewards. But you have to follow the racist White rules, and a large majority of you will never experience, oppression, poverty, injustice, or police brutality—just to name a few—by inheritance of wealth from slavery because of the color of your skin. And if a White person does run into injustice, which is exceedingly rare, the percentage of it is exceptionally low, maybe 1 percent of the White population or less. And how many will lose their life at the hands of law enforcement compared to the loss of Black lives that have been wrongfully murdered by law enforcement officers nationwide?

Now how would you classify that? Is it fair? Is that equal?

I say that is White supremacy at its finest, White world domination! But it will, and it is, coming to an end. The Blacks are just fed up with their lies of deception and deceit, hate, and racism not only in America but the entire world. These racist White supremacists always have to have their hand or face in on everything, and it has to be approved by them; otherwise, it's deemed not good. So once again, do not be fooled by their ways of greed, money, power, and the lust for material things. It is written in the Bible.

If you do not conform to what they consider to be their type of American—and what I mean by that is having to speak properly and act and live like them—then you are considered to be not normal according to their traditional way of life, so they want you to lose your unique identity and become a clone of them so that they can continue their domination of the masses under their control. And if they can control you, they keep total control of the earth—but only for a short amount of time; they know that they are living on borrowed days.

For the Black race to become independent collectively, we must stop depending on them. Because their way of controlling us is vital to them being superior over us. We must become self-sustaining people once again, like in the early 1900s, before integration.

Then we will have control of our own destiny. Do not be foolish enough by continuing to be taking away your hard-earned money to support these so-called stars and celebrities of different races, making them wealthier just for entertainment purposes. They do not care about you; they only care about the money that you spend on them!

And their so-called entertainment and sporting events are nothing more than staged entertainment, which any citizen in America can do with practice. All the while forgetting how they acquired their wealth from the average citizen.

And we need to get the so-called Black leaders who sold us out, out of the way. They will continue to hold their own people back with all of the wealth for themselves attained by so-called Black celebrities, entertainers, politicians, and athletes—who have more than enough wealth to pull their Black race out of poverty in America but are so selfish and greedy that they continue to trick us into thinking that they cannot help their own people, which is a lie. Those are the ones that we need to get out of the way. They must go! They will continue to get richer while the Black people get poorer and stay in the same rut for as long as they can keep us there and prepare us for elimination from the earth.

They would like to continue giving out handouts, having food drives, and warm coats for kids, showing fake concern. And it is done exclusively for the children to show that they really care, which amounts to nothing. So what about the millions of adult Black men and women who do not want handouts but truly need the help and support of the Black wealthy community? No grown person wants a handout; they want to make an honest living and have pride in doing so.

Nothing is mentioned about their condition. They did not choose to be poor. They just happen to be a victim of society, but the ones who have the wealth will come up with all types of reasons as to why they are in the position they are in, and that is a result of slavery and generations of suppressed education, denial of businesses and wealth, and unfair treatment in life in a country who continues to be racist, exactly like their forefathers.

Nothing is wrong with being wealthy, but one has to ask themselves, when does it become greed? Does any one person need hundreds of millions of dollars? And the Black people who do have some wealth rarely help the Black people who are left in disparity, but you want us to continue to support you and praise you as though you are some great human being. You live and die like every single individual that has lived on this earth; you are no different.

Only a few Black people on earth, at a given time, selected by the elite, are able to attain wealth in this world, and they want us to praise them and to think what a big accomplishment they have made to their race and that's supposed to make you feel good, all while they are getting wealthy off of you while you are spending your hard-earned money to see someone that is identical to you, with no special powers, just an average individual like everyone else on earth. The only difference is that they know how they acquired their advantage over their God-fearing counterparts. When you look at the whole situation, it is total manipulation, to keep control of the so-called emancipated Black race.

When we look at the Black race collectively, an exceedingly high majority of us are compassionate, caring, and respectful individuals, regardless of what race we interact with—which we must stop doing and start caring about our own people. Whites and other races, in turn, are very deceitful people, they gain your trust only to stab us in the back. They will lie, cheat, and steal—whatever they can do—to get ahead in life by any means possible, including murder while causing chaos. And they do not care who gets hurt or eliminated in the process, while making it seem as though you are the cause of the problem, trying their best to provoke conflict with a Black person and making themselves out to be so innocent. It is in their nature to be diabolical—not all of them, but an extremely high percentage of them. The proof is in their history, and they cannot deny it.

So the bottom line of this problem is that Whites do not want Black people in this country, but you must think of the mistake they made. For one, you kidnapped our descendants from Alkebulan (the real name of the continent of Africa), then you proclaimed that we are three-fifths of a human being, equal to a field animal, yet were exactly the same as you. So why would you have your White children be breastfed by a Black woman who is considered less than human? How many of your White children were sucking on a Black woman's breast and were raised being nurtured by Black women? Except for the fact that you are a sick race of people, we are one of God's children, too, just like every other race on earth. You still refuse to acknowledge us as human beings. Instead, you treated us like animals and bought and sold us like a commodity. In other words, you treated us like livestock.

Yet the Black race still forgives you for your sins! But remember, we will never *forget* the crimes and damage that you have committed against us as a race of people because we are a creation of the Almighty God too; we only have a different skin color.

When I really contemplate the vast amount of information available now, you have to determine what is true, and the simple answer to that question is this: If you are not Black and if you have never been caught up in a situation where your life is on the line with a revolver pointed in your face, by a so-called unpredictable, racist White peace officer who clearly hates Black people, you'll never be able to comprehend what we've been going through, and that's a fact. So you better not make a sudden move, or your life will be terminated where you stand. It has been done countless times, but they seem to be innocent 99.9 percent of the time.

Have you ever been followed and watched—every move you make, every store you enter—only to be accused of some type of bogus action, or if you go to an appointment and you are greeted as though you have no right being in their place of business? Well, I would not be here if I did not have business to take care of, all the while they are looking at you as if you are crazy and, on top of that, they will become agitated and try to start some kind of conflict to have you removed from the premises. Those are only a few examples of what I have experienced in my adult life, and I could go on and on. But every Black person has to deal with this type of behavior across the nation on a daily basis, and it is very sickening. And it is especially disturbing when they can use your own race against you because then, the sellout Black people think that they are going to gain brownie points with the Caucasian race who do not care one bit about you or me.

Yet they will claim that it is only a few who are like that, which is crap. Look at how our last president, Trump, caused racial division in the four years he was in office. He basically told all of the White racists and White supremacist cowards in America that it is okay to express and show your hate toward Black citizens, and you can do whatever you want to do in the United States of America, including violent behavior.

So now everyone is on the edge, and we do not know what to expect with the new president, lunch box Joe Biden, and personally, he is no better than the one that is leaving the White House! Just a new slave master for us, with the same mentality as the previous presidents in history. If you could only hear what is being said behind closed doors about Black people.

So ask yourself honestly, do you really think he is going to change or reform things in America?

No, as far as I see it, things will be the same, if not worse, when he gets done raping America. We have been fooled for too long. Do not fall for the same promises told to the Black people for decades.

You, White racists, the United States of America will never be able to understand, nor will you experience what the Black race has been going through for centuries, so do not even pretend like you do not know what is going on or act like you care. The gap in your racist healthcare system is just astonishing. And it is just another part of your plot to get rid of the Black race.

The suppression of health care is another way to eliminate the Black man by making it so expensive that only the wealthy can afford quality health care, And look at how many Black men are in poverty. So if you do not have any type of health insurance, you will not be seen by any medical professional, and they do not care if you die!

And from experience, I can tell you that I once tried out a so-called free health clinic, for some medical concerns, at Banner health care, in Arizona, in 2020 because, being uninsured at the time, I thought I could receive some medical assistance. And what I went through was a joke. Not only is the place a racist organization, but they were very nosey, asking questions that had nothing to do with my reason for seeking medical attention, and on top of all of that, prying into my personal medical history. The so-called medical professional thought that disclosing my medical history was funny, so I told them to destroy my personal information and that I no longer would be seeking medical assistance from them. The way I was treated and disrespected, as a Black man, proved that racism is as strong as ever in America against the Black race. So I guess that with me being a Black man, it surprised them that I was concerned about my health. They did not care to make the process smooth for me and only made it extremely difficult and made excuses all the while trying to direct me to someplace else that was just as racist as them.

So in other words, they do not want to treat any Black man who is uninsured, only to make excuses for why they are unable to treat you. So does that sound like a free clinic to you? I call that one big racist joke! So my advice to any Black man who does not have the ability to receive medical care is to take care of your body and to stay away from unhealthy habits, so you will not become one of their guinea pigs on a petri dish.

They will do whatever it takes to try and exterminate you from this planet, so that is why the study of eugenics was created, to continue to develop ways to eliminate the so-called inferior, weak, undesirable class of humans, which they consider the Black race is. That is why the practice of abortion came into play a long time ago, killing Black babies by the millions, up to the present time today. Do your homework, Black America! The creation of fast food is killing us, too, and they know it is addictive, and it is a means to control you so you are being programmed. Change your diet. They have been feeding us garbage for over four hundred years.

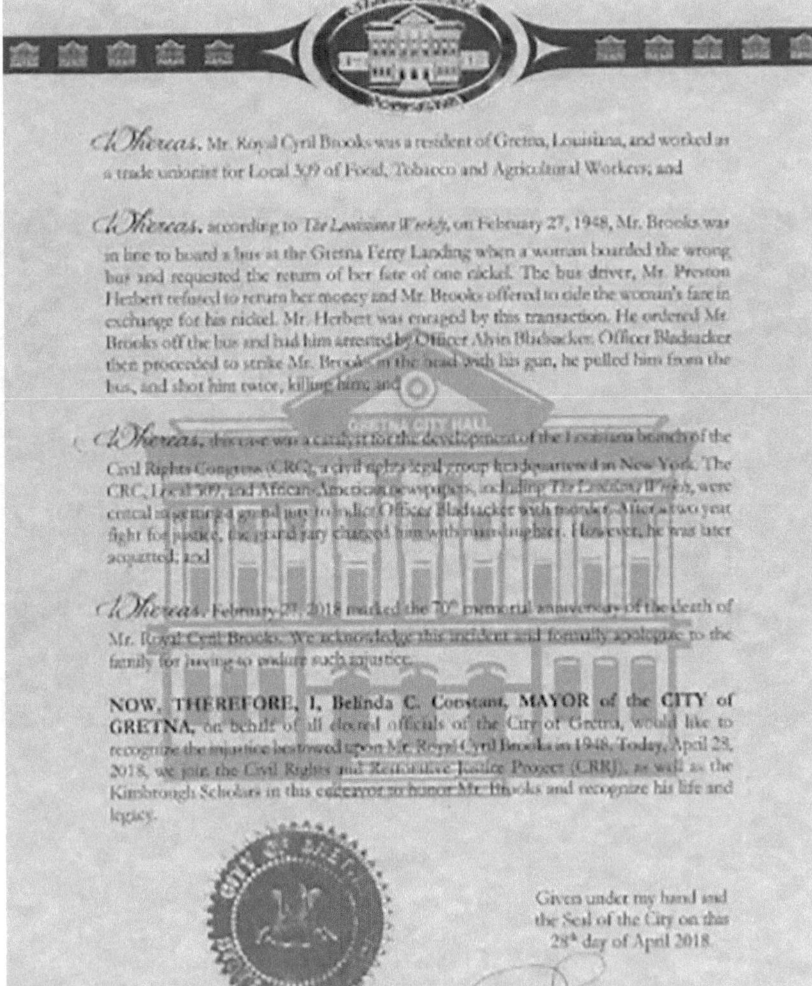

CITY OF GRETNA

Whereas, Mr. Royal Cyril Brooks was a resident of Gretna, Louisiana, and worked as a trade unionist for Local 309 of Food, Tobacco and Agricultural Workers; and

Whereas, according to *The Louisiana Weekly*, on February 27, 1948, Mr. Brooks was in line to board a bus at the Gretna Ferry Landing when a woman boarded the wrong bus and requested the return of her fare of one nickel. The bus driver, Mr. Preston Herbert refused to return her money and Mr. Brooks offered to ride the woman's fare in exchange for his nickel. Mr. Herbert was enraged by this transaction. He ordered Mr. Brooks off the bus and had him arrested by Officer Alvin Bladsacker. Officer Bladsacker then proceeded to strike Mr. Brooks in the head with his gun, he pulled him from the bus, and shot him twice, killing him; and

Whereas, this case was a catalyst for the development of the Louisiana branch of the Civil Rights Congress (CRC), a civil rights legal group headquartered in New York. The CRC, Local 309, and African American newspapers, including *The Louisiana Weekly*, were critical in getting a grand jury to indict Officer Bladsacker with murder. After a two year fight for justice, the grand jury charged him with manslaughter. However, he was later acquitted; and

Whereas, February 27, 2018 marked the 70th memorial anniversary of the death of Mr. Royal Cyril Brooks. We acknowledge this incident and formally apologize to the family for having to endure such injustice.

NOW, THEREFORE, I, Belinda C. Constant, **MAYOR** of the **CITY** of **GRETNA**, on behalf of all elected officials of the City of Gretna, would like to recognize the injustice bestowed upon Mr. Royal Cyril Brooks in 1948. Today, April 28, 2018, we join the Civil Rights and Restorative Justice Project (CRRJ), as well as the Kimbrough Scholars in this endeavor to honor Mr. Brooks and recognize his life and legacy.

Given under my hand and the Seal of the City on this 28th day of April 2018.

MAYOR

The original declaration from the present day mayor
of the city of Gretna, La. Belinda C. Constant.

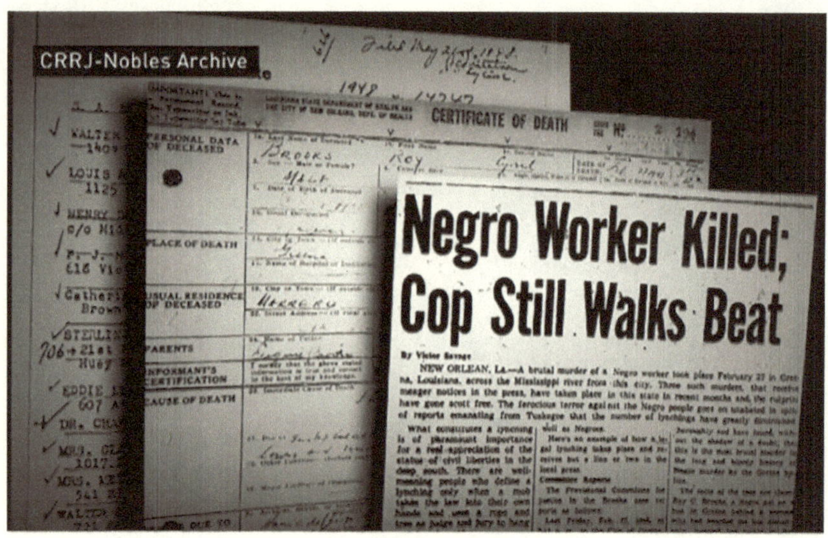

Royal Cyril Brooks 1903–1948

CHAPTER 2

Truth or Trickery

So as long as they can continue to trick you by limiting the amount of knowledge you have about the diabolical agendas that they have going on in their laboratories, we will be at their mercy, and with the help of the handpicked Black people, who are paid to keep their own people in the crab barrel, we will always be stuck in a rut. Those are the Black people who have the same mentality as the Black people who sold many of our descendants into slavery. They are descendants of the sellouts because they will do anything for a dollar for their slave masters, even if it means selling out their own race!

It is so much going on it's mind-boggling, and I do not understand why our own people, the Negroes with a little education—except for a few—will not tell the rest of us the truth of their hidden agendas. So I guess they will take their secrets to the grave. Until every Black person knows the truth behind America's plan, we are doomed, except for the hand-picked Negroes who will serve their slave masters and protect their slave masters' secret to the end, just for mere coins.

So we must put the creator of human life, the Almighty God first and foremost because he is the only one that can put an end to this deliberate madness and bring peace to the earth because the darkness that they are doing has been brought to the light.

Every Black person must continue to get educated and realize that as a race, we can try and repair the damage that has been done to our race, and when we truly know who we are, things will get better. And instead of fighting and killing each other over man-made material things, we need to reorganize and try to be more civil toward one another, because we are doing what they want us to do, making their job easier for them, and that is eliminating our own selves over foolishness.

We must realize that as God's children, it is important to maintain focus and to keep your faith and that all the problems in the world today cannot and will not be solved by man. If it is answers and solutions that we seek, all of the answers are in the word of God, in his powerful book, the Holy Bible!

Do not be tricked by believing that the government or man has the answers or solutions to what is going on in the world today. That is why it is in the shape that it is in, which is turmoil.

Now another deception in this country is this: They try and continue to emasculate the weak-minded Black man through manipulation and deception for fame and fortune. How? I will explain some of the facts as I see them. By getting these confused individuals, which many of them have been molested as a child, to publicly admit that they are proud of their altered orientation, you are going against the word of the Almighty God. Don't get it twisted. I'm not the judge of the decisions that you make in life. It's your choice, but you will have to explain to the Almighty God, our Heavenly Father, about the lifestyle that you have chosen because he is waiting patiently to judge every man and woman of the sins that have been committed on earth.

Okay, they try their best to feminize the Black man by dressing up as a woman or wearing women's clothing and make-up, by telling us that it is okay, it is just for entertainment purposes or an expression of freedom, which is an abomination in God's eyes. But what you don't tell in your sick perverted history and in your textbooks is what disturbed slave masters called buck breaking, and that is when slave masters whipped a slave into exhaustion and submission and then proceeded to rape a grown man in front of all of the slaves and even their women and children so that the Black man would be humiliated and disrespected by other slaves and looked upon as less than a man. And other slave owners in the area would join in on the sadistic ritual, so that was a very disturbed and sick practice.

You have brainwashed the Black women and the other races to degrade and demoralize, disrespect, and bash the Black man, regardless of our contributions to humankind and the world.

Continuing to try and destroy our image and family structure, like the chaos you caused during the time of slavery, when we were denied the God-given right to be husbands to our wives and fathers to our kids. Just like how you took the very right away from Royal Cyril Brooks to be a husband to his wife and a father to his children. Many Black men have fallen for this sinful deception, because of the manipulation and trickery for fame and fortune. I will not mention names, but they know who they are.

Now this is what bothers me a lot about their agenda to disrespect the Black man and children of this country: As hard and dedicated as our Black male youths, putting in hours and days of practice, trying to become the best athletes that they could become, I could not believe that during the half time show during the Super Bowl 2021, I could not understand why they would give an award for skills and abilities in a sport for males—and where Black males make up the majority of professional football players—to a little Black girl, knowing that she will never play organized professional men's football. So out of all of the diligent Black male youths in the nation, you mean to tell me that the little Black girl was a better-skilled player than the little Black male youth players who put in God knows how many hours of practice, in all kinds of weather? Okay, that is one of the main reasons why I stopped watching all of their staged sporting events on television! So why are they trying to integrate women into men's sports, and vice versa, where Black people are superior?

If you cannot read between the lines, you ought to seek help. A subliminal message is meant to mess with our minds as Black men. And that is just one of their many ways of humiliating us, along with a multitude of deceptions that they have placed in the Black community. Telling us that it is okay to go against the Almighty God's will, their sick perverted ways will send you to the lake of fire. Do not go against God's law of life for humankind.

What did they really mean when written in their own words that everyone was equal?

It was part of their deception, getting the Black race to honestly believe that after being treated like grazing animals, they would consider us equal to them. Since the so-called emancipation of the Black race, economic racism and inequality ways continue to destroy the Black family structure; generations of poverty, the target of their sick experiments, and their continuation of the elimination of the Black race through disease and poison.

So do you honestly think that we would genuinely believe anything you would say to us after centuries of bondage, killings, and all types of unimaginable treatment, even to this very day? But you do have certain Black people, that for some strange reason, do believe you, thinking that you have changed your sick behavior, which has been passed down over the many generations.

Your sickness has plagued you since the beginning of time, a vast majority of you are descendants of infected blood, and you have pure hate inside of you, pumping through your veins.

And the disturbing part is that you are still trying to convince the world that you stand for peace and equality yet you continue to dominate the world with control of the most valuable resources that you have stolen from other countries and the deadly, violent, and very destructive weapons that you have produced—that proves your violent nature—to maintain control of the earth, along with wealth, to stay superior against any race. And you will annihilate anyone that opposes you.

So by keeping the masses blind to your secret agenda by limiting their education and twisting the history books and keeping them in poverty and sickness and illness with lack of medical care and an extremely poor diet consisting of fast food and consuming vast amounts of alcohol, cigarettes, and drugs, it becomes extremely hard for them to believe the truth when it is told to them because their attention is focused on the distractions of material things that you have made—money, cars, clothes, electronic gadgets and the really bad things: fast food, drugs, alcohol, cigarettes, unclean music, and movies—all designed to destroy us, because the few things that I just mentioned are made for us to kill another human being over, which is nonsense, and that's exactly what they want.

And it is especially present in the Black families and neighborhoods after centuries of poverty and no hope of improvement in their lives because of the repercussions of slavery, which was done by deliberate design. So ask yourselves, do you think we can trust any of you and the Black people that are working for you?

Now another part of their trickery is to not only hold us underwater but to have handpicked Negroes keep the majority of Blacks in poverty by feeding us lies, trying to convince us that they are about fairness, equality, and truth and justice, but all the while, setting their own race up for the kill. They have a big price to pay when it is time to face the Almighty God.

You have been lying to the Black race for an exceedingly long time, and until we, the Black race, wake up and realize that we are being treated like modern-day slaves, we will never be independent and will always be held in the crab barrel.

I do not see anything getting better in this country soon, it seems like everything is spinning in one big circle, and that is what they want, to keep us confused.

It is so much to be told that I will never have enough words to explain what is happening in America today. Some will claim that I'm ranting, but in the future, when my book is read, you will realize that everything I'm writing about is the truth, but it will be too late to stand up for your human rights. It's what the Almighty God has given mankind from the beginning, but the ones that are in control didn't listen, and now we are the victims of them being disobedient to the Almighty God.

We, as a people, are being fooled and brainwashed.

Believe in the Almighty God; do not go to hell.

What is happening in America is a slow process of self-destruction concerning greed and money. All you have to do is look very closely at the current events, which are happening all over the country and in the world. It is in ruins. And the only way to get some sense of sanity is to seek the help of the Almighty God. But the government will not bring God in on the problems, and during the pandemic, I have not heard any so-called political leader mention the Almighty God's name. So they will continue to keep the masses distracted and disoriented by using blatant racism and injustice to their advantage, so the Black race must continue to strive for equality and economic fairness.

Current events of rebellion and crime are propaganda made up by the government, staged acts to arouse the masses to react in an abnormal way which results in violent behavior and rioting. So they will continue to inject this false sense of information to get the desired results—which is total chaos—to keep the people of this country's minds off of the key issues, which would be racial injustice and economic inequality while keeping the Black race in the same position as 150 years ago and many years before.

Now that the country is trying to recover from the rioting, from coast to coast, the same thing is starting to erupt once again. Police nationwide are continuing to use deadly force on Black citizens who are accused of committing weak infractions of the law while protesters are having brutal clashes with law enforcement and police officers are killing Black men and assaulting us on a weekly basis. So if we are being treated in a manner of a subhuman, imagine what Royal Cyril Brooks went through in Louisiana.

The judicial system in the state of Louisiana in 1948 was a joke and an extremely racist, White-run government during that time—and even today—and had the mindset that Black people are still inferior human beings and would never be equal to them. So in their eyes and in the eyes of White America, we will always be a class of sub-humans and will be kept in that position.

So many Black lives were lost throughout the beginning of America due to racial injustice and hate of the Black race. That is why Royal Cyril Brooks, my grandfather, did not receive a fair trial after he was murdered in the street by a cowardly law enforcement officer, even though there were hundreds of eyewitnesses, and the so-called judge who presided over my grandfather's murder case was a jasper—just straight racist. But I would like you to remember this fact: Two thousand people attended Royal Cyril Brooks's funeral.

How can a racist White government, acquit anyone for shooting an unarmed man in the back? I do not care if it was a law enforcement officer; he committed a deadly, cowardly act toward a defenseless, unarmed Black human being, shooting him at point-blank range in the back and in his side.

So how was that justifiable homicide? How was he able to get away with slaying a Black man in broad daylight? And he knew that he was going to get away with it! Exactly like in the days of slavery, you could kill a Black man if you were White and get away with murder without fear of consequences and no questions asked because of the color of your skin.

That is extreme racism displayed by the state government of Louisiana and by the police department of the very racist city of Gretna, Louisiana, as well as the unbalanced injustice of the state of Louisiana judicial system, which falls under the umbrella of the United States government. And I cannot forget how the American federal government turned its back against my grandfather, Royal Cyril Brooks, more than seventy years ago and let that police officer get away with murdering my grandfather, free and clear.

It's that injustice and racism and everything that comes with it, and I am still waiting for these so-called Black leaders of the American people to comment on this major atrocity committed against my grandfather.

So how can you have trust in a system that is corrupted and racist, when a crime as obvious as this was hidden from American history for more than seventy years.

Where are the people, of all races, who claim that they are against injustice and racism, but they continue to tell the same old stories, year in and out, of injustice, which everyone knows about because it is pounded in the citizens' heads of America, but they never mention the true and new stories about racism that are discovered through research. It seems as though they want to forget the past and continue to insert the same old stories in our minds so that we do not think of anything else. I cannot respect nor support the racist government or law enforcement in the state of Louisiana who clearly had a hand in the murder of my grandfather, Royal Cyril Brooks, by letting that police officer get away with first-degree murder. I am not one to just say, "That is okay;" it is not that easy, especially when you look at the facts and the photo from 1948 of my granddad lying in the street in a pool of blood, with my uncle sitting on the curb next to him and plenty of eyewitnesses in the photo staring at my grandfather's lifeless body, and the police officer is nowhere in the photo, nowhere in sight. He did not even stay on the scene.

What kind of human being was that police officer? They say a picture is worth a thousand words, well, look at the photo that was captured in 1948, in Gretna, Louisiana, at the ferry landing bus stop moments after my grandfather, Royal Cyril Brooks, was murdered, shot down like an animal in the street.

I guess I'm supposed to be like, "Oh, that is okay. The White police officer was just doing his job." Bull. You can never tell me that he did his job, as far as I am concerned. He brutally and violently murdered my grandfather in cold blood, in broad daylight. A racist system protected him, a racist White supremacist—an unprofessional, unstable, poorly trained cop—from the punishment of their own written United States of America law.

And I will forever be hurt by how my grandfather was disrespected and treated in this country. The pain will last forever in the Brooks family. We will never forget how our grandfather was disrespected and murdered, yet you expect people to respect the law enforcement in this country. Give me one good reason why I should trust your so-called racist White law enforcement and judicial system?

If the picture was not taken moments after my grandfather was killed by that police officer, there would be doubt. And it is extremely rare that a photograph is captured when one of their law enforcement officers has killed another Black human being in 1948. Even though one of their own racist White police officers tried to destroy the photographer's camera, while trying to destroy the picture, he could not. And my question is, how was a photographer able to be in the area at the time when my grandfather was murdered? And he was able to get the photograph. Was it divine intervention? Even with all of the eyewitnesses, the police officer went home to his family, innocent of murder and able to enjoy his life as a free man, while the Brooks had to bury their father, and at the time, Royal Cyril Brooks' youngest son, Herman L. Brooks (my father), had to come home from the military to his father's funeral, and he had just enlisted six months earlier. What awful news to get, that your father has been murdered over the dispute of a five-cent bus fare.

I have this to say, and I challenge the government of the United States and any lawyer or judge in America to tell me that being unarmed and not committing any crime can justify any law enforcement officer shooting anyone in the back; that it could be called justifiable homicide. Murder has been committed, and a racist system protected that police officer from prosecution of their written law!

That incident, seen by the eyes of the Almighty God, was pure evil, racism, injustice, and total disrespect for human life. And your apologies do not mean anything to me because you let that police officer get away with what I see as a premeditated first-degree homicide.

Where was the justice? Where was the honesty? Where was the fairness? There was not any, not one bit!

I tell you this, it was one big display of White supremacists having their way in one corrupted racist White city, and the racist White United States government in 1948 did not care about the racism that the Black citizens had to endure during that era in America. But you want every Black citizen in the United States to be loyal to your government, and if not, you are a threat. But you have law enforcement being a threat to the Black man when you can kill us at your own will.

So I have to say that we are dealing with some disturbed individuals, according to their law, to call the murder of Royal Cyril Brooks, unarmed, a justifiable homicide, when he was shot in the spine. Better yet, you tell me. What would you call it? Now the use of words is another way to trick your thinking process. Why do you think words look like the thing that they are designed to describe, and how you react to certain situations is directed by selectively placing designed word usage into laws, and in school textbooks? How? I will give you an example and you be the judge.

Someone is in the hospital for a disease, illness, or injury, right? So you are treated by a medical professional—which I have no problem with, and a remarkably high percentage of them know exactly what they are doing by the gift of the Almighty God.

But this is what makes them some of the most arrogant and disrespectful and racist people on the planet: Because of the work that they perform, if the procedure or treatment is successful, the first thing that someone says is, "Thank you. You saved my life."

But in reality, you should be saying, "Thank you for prolonging my life," or "extending my longevity a little longer on earth."

See the word usage we have been taught as a child to think that doctors can save lives, which is false. Only the Almighty God, Lord and Savior Jesus Christ can save lives. Because if your doctors saved lives, they would be ridding you of sin, and they would never lose a patient that they have attempted to prolong on earth. I do not know exactly how long this saying has been used, but I know it has been used for an extremely long time. Also, a doctor does not live longer than the patients they care for medically. A doctor can only prolong or extend your life; they cannot save your life. No person can save a life. Now you know how word usage can trick you, by confusing the meaning of words, and how words are used. That is what makes doctors big-headed and the most conceited people in the world, who think that they are better than everyone. Do not be tricked. That saying has been fooling the masses for a long time. *Saved* is confused with the word *rescued* also.

Remember that words can have various meanings and are enormously powerful when combined into phrases that are meant to confuse a person with limited education. So it is critically important that we continue to stress the importance of education to our younger Black generation, especially to the poverty-stricken Black children. That is why slaves were forbidden to read and write so that the White race can continue to be superior to us. Now do you know why they continue to make education a big issue, and expensive, which falls into the category of injustice, inequality, and racism?

By making higher education so costly, it deters the Black race from seeking increased knowledge of the world, and if you are poorly educated and in poverty, you will have a challenging task in front of you to acquire a good education, along with racist instructors who do not care if you learn anything, but if you are bright, gifted, and extremely intelligent, they will place distractions, obstacles, and all types of excuses to make it difficult, to keep you from achieving your goal, which is getting your degree.

Racism and social injustice have many branches to keep the Black race from reaching equality in this country, which is why there are so many different steps and departments concerning the issue.

How can Blacks receive justice in the United States of America when the government refuses to face the truth? Will they ever admit that this is a racist country, created by the bloodshed of tens of thousands of Black human beings? And the only thing that it is doing is sending you to a premature grave, from your worrying and the abundance of the stress of not knowing how the next day will be. So the suppression of education is one of their secret tricks to keeping racism and injustice alive. If you have doubt, take a look at the number of Black enrollments in colleges and universities across the country.

So we move on to another major topic which lies in every Black neighborhood in America, and that is the structure of the American government. It was designed to keep the Black race in an inferior position by electing racist lawmakers who continue to create laws that affect the very life of the Black race every day.

Those are the ones—the elected officials who are groomed from an early age to keep White supremacy alive and strong. They will never let you see their true colors, nor will you be told the truth as to why there are so many different laws on the books.

I seriously doubt that you need all of the laws that America has that were created on lawmakers' tables to control a nation, yet there are thousands of laws designed to inflict fear in a certain group of people, which is directed at Black people. If it were not made for you, why does it seem like the Black race and other people of color are the only ones breaking their law, but the White race rarely gets accused of the very same laws that they have made.

Well, if you have doubt, take a look at who is filling up the penitentiaries—the Black men and other people of color. Racist sentencing guidelines and unfair judges both Black and White nationwide continue to violate Black men's and women's rights by handing out unjust punishments while hiding their racist ways. Also, these low-level public defenders do not care if you are sentenced unjustly because they are paid to get you locked up for as long as the unfair law allows.

So now, in modern times, we have to deal with the racist Black officials, descendants of the sellouts, and members of these secret fraternities and sororities who are elected and appointed by design, to oppress their own people in order to deflect the racism away from the Whites that are in power, leaving them time to work on more diabolical plots against the Black race.

And that is a disturbing fact, to have your own race working to hold you back. Those are the worst Black people, that will sell their souls for power and a few coins, only to be sentenced to total damnation.

These sellout Black people who hate their own race of Black people are in all aspects of the country. They are placed strategically, throughout the government, law enforcement, and judicial systems, as well as medical professionals and educators, where they are a serious threat to not only our wellbeing but to our very own survival on this planet until they get the desired amount of Black people on earth that would be acceptable to them. Then it will be a much easier job, controlling us, keeping us in one place, under manageable numbers, under their control, and it will be easier for them to exterminate us whenever they feel like it, without having to hunt us down all over the country or the world.

That is how the government is set up to keep social injustice flowing and using our own race against us. So they will definitely use our own kind as puppets in keeping racism and injustice alive.

And now I have to touch base on law enforcement in this country, which we already know have some key issues going on. Law enforcement in the United States of America has always been racist toward the Black race, and the corrupted law enforcement, which I call the blue organization, goes by a secret code of conduct— that all police departments, sheriff's offices, and all of the other law enforcement agencies follow nationwide, including the Black officers and female police officers of all races who have been specifically brainwashed and trained to follow orders—to corral Black men and people of color, to get them out of society, and to put it plainly, incarcerate you in their human zoo. And they are programmed to kill you, even if you are a Black woman, if you put up the slightest resistance. All you have to do is look at the number of unarmed Black civilian police killings in this country, along with life-altering felony assaults against the Black race. It has been done since the beginning of slavery. Their racist White law enforcement in the United States of America, in 1838, was the creation of the first racist White police or blue organization in Boston, Massachusetts, before the end of slavery. But the origin was during the time of slavery when they had the patty rollers, which the slaves called paddy rollers (and that is where the term *paddy wagon* comes from), plantation police whose specific job was to keep Black people from leaving the property of the slave owners without permission, and if they were caught without a slave owner's documentation of movement, the consequences would be severe, which included death. And that is the main purpose of law enforcement today, to keep Black people under control and to keep you in these extremely dangerous cities and towns, away from their communities. With that mentality, power was given to these police officers, of which many are very unstable individuals with multiple dysfunctions and mental reasoning problems nationwide. They were given the authority from a very racist, White government, the legal right to murder anyone that opposes their manufactured law or government. And not one human being in the United States can protest or denounce their created law—which they made according to their rule, but they did not follow God's law of man.

So the result as we know it today is total chaos and madness, and out-of-control crime from coast to coast, with injustice and racism at an all-time high, which once again, was done by deliberate design. And by that, Royal Cyril Brooks became a victim of their injustice because of the immunity that was given to their so-called honest peace officer.

Now remember what I told you about words and phrases, and how powerful they can be when combined together to confuse their meaning? Take a close look at these titles—*officer*, once *overseer*. See how closely they are related, and their jobs are the same. The overseer patrolled the plantation, and the officer patrols the nation. How ironic that both jobs are the same. Their main focus of attention is directed at the Black race, particularly the Black man.

So as you can read what I am saying, an officer is nothing more than a disguised, modern-day overseer put in place by the United States government to keep control of the Black race, which is why the interactions are always so brutal and violent. Because they have the same mentality that the Black race is still inferior human beings and will never be equal to the White race, it is their job to maintain control of us, as in the past total domination of the Black race.

Until all of these corrupted, dishonest, and White supremacist police officers, judges, and government officials, and many of the sellout Black people, which are no better, are weeded out of the country's law enforcement and the judicial government system, there will never be equal justice; only more lives taken and lies being told to protect them from prosecution.

And the first thing that they will say is that it is only a few, but we all know that it is far more than a few. So how were they clever enough to slip past your process of hiring? Something is wrong with your system, and you do not find out until after the fact that they are racist killers.

And I guarantee that many more crimes including unsolved murders of Black men have been committed by your so-called hero police officers nationwide, but you forgot that the eyes of the Almighty God have been watching everything that you do.

So law enforcement will continue to do their dirty work for the government, and this fake talk of reform is nothing but talk. You may think that they are going to reform law enforcement, but you are in for a massive surprise. Maybe when they feel like when it is in their best interest.

They are in no hurry to change what has been working for law enforcement against the Black race for over a century and a half because of some protesters. Look what happened when people were protesting in the sixties. They got beaten down and murdered. They passed a few bogus laws to pacify so-called sellout black leaders to make it seem like they were really doing something for the Black race, but we are doing the same thing today, and nothing is getting done. You might as well stay at home and protest on your computer. And if you do not believe what I am saying, listen to this: Look how long it took for them to abolish slavery, look how long it took for the Black race to get so-called civil rights, only for those same rights to be transferred to diverse groups who had nothing to do with slavery or so-called civil rights, which was specifically made for Black people. Now how long do you think it is going to take for them to reform the law enforcement, judicial system, and the government lawmakers, who continue making ridiculous laws, every year. Now look how much of the taxpayers' money is being wasted by the government on nonsense.

So if they can get you to believe that, you have just been tricked once again, and the laws that they have created back in history are the exact same laws that they continue to break to this very day. Wake up, Black America and other people of color!

Now I will make this statement, this is how corrupted the police are in Milwaukee, Wisconsin.

My wife was the victim of an attempted robbery in December 2017. One afternoon, she was walking to the bank while I was at work, and a man attacked her, trying to snatch her up to go into her pockets to rob her. She fought back, and luckily, she ran into a nearby auto dealership, and they scared the assailant away. She reported it to the Milwaukee, Wisconsin, police department. They told her that they would come to our residence in a few hours. They never showed up. We waited a whole week. They never did a follow-up. So in other words, they did not care or performed their job as a public servant. I could not believe it! I was furious. That was not only disrespectful and unprofessional, I know for a fact that they neglected to look into the attempted robbery and the assault of my wife, and I have no respect for them. And that is why my wife and I relocated from that racist city. And I have many more stories of how they failed to perform their duty as law enforcement.

But put the shoe on the other foot. Had it been their wife or one of their family members, they would have hunted that criminal down and would have beaten the assailant to the ground or killed him. This is the kind of law enforcement that we have to deal with all across the nation—dirty individuals with no morals or feelings for the Black race.

We are only a target of their racial profiling, and they think that everyone that is Black is the suspect or criminal. Whether you are dressed in a business suit or in a sweat suit, if you are accused of any type of wrongdoing or committing a crime, especially if you are of the Black race, they are coming to beat you down and take you to jail, and if things get out of control, you may just lose your life. And these police officers do not care about any Black adult, especially the female Black police officers—they hate Black men with a passion. Why do you think that so many of them have become law enforcement officers? They will stay loyal and dedicated to each other all the way to the end. That is how the Milwaukee police department conducts its business in the Black community. And look at their history of killing unarmed Black men. And I can speak on it because if you read about the killing of Daniel Bell in the 1950s in Milwaukee, Wisconsin.

That was my cousin, so America is a very racist and deadly country for the Black man. So it is very disturbing that my grandfather, Royal Cyril Brooks, was murdered by police in Gretna, Louisiana, on February 28, 1948, and a thousand miles away, in Milwaukee, Wisconsin, my cousin was murdered ten years later in the same month, on February 2, 1958, by a racist White city of Milwaukee police officer. See the pattern of racism, injustice, and the murdering of unarmed Black men?

So take a good look at the violent history that this country's law enforcement has done against the Brooks bloodline. Documented facts. My cousin was executed the same as my grandfather. Daniel was shot at point-blank range in the back of his neck while lying on the ground. So it is a terrible trend that these Black men were shot and murdered from behind, by so-called heroic and honest police officers.

And once again, these police officers have been doing these killings for an extremely long time, and they are not going to change their ways overnight. It will take tens of decades for them to even consider change. But you want us to praise them like they are great human beings.

So this is what gets me: They will tell you how much restraint these police officers have, but in reality, the only thing that is on their minds is to kill anyone that doesn't obey their command. Who are you to tell anyone to follow your command? You are human just like us, and if we do not obey your command, you can shoot to kill—not tase, but kill—with deadly force because you feel as though you have superior authority over the civilian population. But remember that everyone must obey the law.

When people become law enforcement officers in their blue organization, they become different. They look at every Black person as a suspect; their authority goes to their head. Then when any one of them is lost in the line of duty, they tell how honest and dedicated and caring they were. But they will never tell you the truth of how they really were as a person. How can every single one of them be good people? They are like every single person on earth. They were sinners. They only want to speak of the so-called good that they have done but never the bad—and you better believe it was plenty of bad done too. Otherwise, they would not have lost their lives in the line of duty, which the Almighty God had it that way.

You want sympathy and praise from everyone, trying your best to convince the Black race that you performed such an excellent job for the community and that you were a great, heroic police officer. But you could have been the worst racist police officer on the police force, White or Black, and you definitely cannot get me to shed a tear for any of you after the way my grandfather Royal Cyril Brooks was violently and brutally murdered by one of your fellow brother police officer and the countless number of innocent Black men who have died by the hands of law enforcement, only to be forgotten after they were buried.

But you want your racist, unfair, crooked police officers to be remembered by having memorials and dedication ceremonies, to show that their job was superior to all, and that just turns my stomach.

I am through because they are a joke.

Here lies Royal Cyril Brooks.

CHAPTER 3

Racism, Research, Experimentation, Elimination (RREE)

Racism, research, and experimentation go together with elimination. Back in history, we all remember the Tuskegee experiment, and I do not know if my father was a part of your sick and diabolical testing because he joined your racist armed forces in 1947, in the state of Louisiana, one state away from the state of Alabama. So why is the government so vigilant for the Black race to get an experimental COVID-19 vaccination, which is starting to kill off people, worse than the virus itself. Is it because we are at the bottom of society, because we have less income, or because they consider us an inferior race of humans? Is it their secret agenda of eugenics and depopulation? Along with the elimination of the Black race? Yes, it is a designed plan, staged by racist White world leaders, with the racist White American government leading the charge.

Wake up, Black citizens! Do not be tricked! Do not go to hell, I am telling you now! The mark of the beast is in full effect, and it is just the beginning. We have been warned by honest and truthful clergy and religious leaders and Black doctors and scholars who know the real truth, but we have not paid close attention to the warnings given to humankind, and now it is here. So you can go ahead and get a mark of the beast vaccination, by coercion, and by them playing some old song to get into your feelings.

By letting these so-called Black politicians, celebrities, and entertainers, who are paid to convince you that it is safe and effective, but I ask you this, how do you know that they have received it themselves? Did you actually see a bottle, taken from a case containing the actual vaccination that they have taken? Do you honestly think that the so-called vaccination that the wealthy is getting is the same as the general population? How do you know it was the actual vaccination serum taken by so-called celebrities? How do you know that the vaccine being delivered to the Black neighborhoods is the same as in the White communities? Do you know exactly what they are putting in these vaccines? There is documentation of deadly consequences and severe levels of impairment from not only taking the COVID-19 vaccine but all manufactured vaccinations.

How do you know if it was not just a placebo shot that they were getting? Why would you let them inject a deadly virus into you, if you are already a healthy adult, and you are not infected? I tell you, they want to infect you and to see if you have any underlying health issues, and if you do have any type of weak internal organs, they know through research that the fabricated COVID-19 will kill you. So is that depopulation of the weak?

Look at their history of deception. Look at the Black people that work for them, that will sell you out. Look at the catastrophic damage that they did to the Tuskegee Airmen, and you are trying your best to convince me that it is safe and that I can trust you, and I need it in order to reenter your White-run racist society or to board any of your racist commercial transportation or to go to one of your restaurants? It is okay if I go to a fast-food restaurant unvaccinated, but I have to show proof of vaccination to attend any of your staged sporting events or concerts? And if I do not have your mark of the beast vaccination card, I cannot participate in any of your adored, so-called social community events? Or you will charge a ridiculous price for service if I am not vaccinated.

That is straight racism and discrimination directed at the Black people, but they have made it the law because of their manufactured plague and their mandatory requirements in order to travel the country or to go abroad in the world. And they are solely concerned, with the Black population and other races of color getting this injection? So tell me this, why do you rarely see commercials, stressing the fact for the White population to get vaccinated? Why do you seldom see any Caucasian celebrities, or anyone of that nature, saying that the vaccine is important to their race?

Because they are not getting it. I will never believe any of your so-called, doctors, politicians, athletes, or entertainers! Because they have tricked the Black race into thinking that we can trust them once again to get a vaccination because they say that it is safe and that we can trust them. How? Because they say so, and that they are honest. Tell me this, how can you trust anyone that has sold their soul? Knowing that their eternal life is lost, by doing the work of the elite.

Everything that I have tried to explain to the masses has been ignored, but it is up to you to pay attention and believe the truth. My personal and very realistic statement is this: You can get the vaccination at your own risk. But remember, they have tricked you into getting a vaccine that has never been evaluated properly for less than a year of testing. So if you or any of your family members die from severe side effects of being injected with a deadly virus that they barely know anything about, you will not be able to hold them liable, because you took it of your own free will. So be prepared for the next life-altering step, and that is the microchip! They already have your information because you have to register your vaccination card to show proof that you are vaccinated, so you are automatically tracked. When you enter that information on your cell phone, they know who you are, and they know where you are and have all of your personal identification.

Now the experimentation of the Black race is nothing new to White supremacy. The countries of England and France have countless of numbers of documented history of conducting their Frankenstein-type experimentations against the Black race, dating back to the mid-1700s, so who do you think they have been using up to the present time? And who do you think are they using secretly in their experiments now? Do you honestly think that they have stopped using the Black race in their disturbing experiments, while you are distracted with their manufactured material things? And the experimenting with the Black prison population is a reality also.

Not paying attention to what is going on in this country will definitely get the Black race exterminated from this planet, along with the sellout Black people, who will become the future slaves. God knows what they will do to keep from being decimated along with the rest of the Black population. Listen, the manipulation that they have going on is meant to fool an average individual, just like you, into thinking that you can believe them and trust them, just because they have fame and fortune. If you do, you are a weak-minded person. You cannot fool me into your voluntary experimentation of depopulation through the deception of research and poisoning, along with a record of killing scores of human beings.

These experimentations and testing are conducted on the masses every day through the products and food that they introduce to the public daily, and whatever the masses attach to, then they will continue to pump that poison into the country nonstop, and it is in fast food, cosmetics, and the products that you use for daily hygiene.

And the extremely terrible research conducted against the Black youth by strategically placing tobacco and liquor stores, by design, in our poverty-stricken neighborhoods. It has been going on for an exceedingly long time, along with highly addictive drugs, which are meant to shorten your life. See, they already know the damage that will be done, if you combine all of these substances over a very long period. It will definitely have an adverse and severe effect on an especially important internal organ, the heart, along with severe damage to the brain and unrepairable damage to other major organs, and that is when they will continue their experimentations to find out what you can combine, and what not to as far as substances and chemicals go. Now if the experiments are facts of what to use and what effects they have on human beings, how can you not use human test subjects, even to this very day?

Now the invention of the so-called technological electronic devices has been a tool to cause damage to the mind, and to have you become addicted to cell phones, video games, televisions, computers, and microwave ovens is a way to have you distracted from the reality of life by taking away the proper functioning of your brain by using electrical impulses caused by the use of these devices. All of the electronics that I have mentioned, and an abundance of many more, have been researched by the government, and they know for a fact, through research, that continued use of them over an extended period of time will damage and alter your brain, which is why television is so hard not to watch, and you cannot put that cell phone down. Also, the use of microwave ovens is dramatically altering the food that we consume, and it is especially hard to get your children from putting down their video games and picking up a book. These children will play these games all day and night if allowed, so what would you call that? Addiction? Manipulation, distraction, and deception?

And the Black race is being fooled once again. You will buy your kids an expensive video game, cell phone, or television, instead of encouraging them to pick up a book or having them engage in some outdoor activity or something that naturally stimulates the mind and challenges them to think without the use of so many electronic devices. That is why we have an obesity problem in this country, by design.

These video games can cause documented epileptic seizures by exposure to the constant flashing of assorted colors of light.

That is a manipulation of the mind while introducing your kids to extreme violence and pornography, secretly causing damage to the proper thinking process, without even realizing it. So now we will have a generation of young people with all sorts of brain disorders, unable to think on their own correctly, and will have a tough time distinguishing reality from fantasy. Then they will start to conduct new experiments, with the test subjects being the Black race once again.

So as you can read, the government has all types of ways and experiments of keeping the Black race suppressed, and as long as they can keep you distorted and distracted, they can continue to use racism and injustice against you because your mind is concentrating on what is coming on television, or "I need to buy that new video game," or "Who is going to call or text me on my cell phone?" and so on. And while you are being disoriented and distracted, you do not even realize what they have been doing, and that is plotting your elimination from this earth, preparing it for their children, without them having to see too many Black faces in society, if any, in the future.

They will continue to use all types of vaccines, telling you that you need them, in order to survive on this planet, which is false information. Man has been on this earth for an awfully long time, before the man-made creation of their so-called vaccinations, which are different from certain medicines which treat you with disease and illness. So they use this as a means to secretly depopulate the earth, and by making it a race thing, you have to ask yourself, What does race have to do with getting a fabricated virus injected into your body?

These deviant scientists have been plotting ways to eliminate the Black race for centuries, and they are not about to stop now. They have had centuries of practice to perfect their experiments against the Black race, and now they are finally succeeding. So Black America needs to watch very closely about the agenda of their manufactured vaccines, which are designed to kill you slowly, during your lifetime or within a few years, depending on your immune system, or it will make you incapacitated to where you cannot function properly or independently in society.

And now once they get the majority of the Black adult population infected with this virus, the next target is the Black children, by infecting a generation from growing up as healthy adults—which the percentages will be catastrophic, because a lot of them will not see adulthood, or they will become physically challenged all of their lives. Can the government tell us the truth about how many people are really dying or becoming incapacitated from their supposedly safe vaccines? They will never give an accurate number, but they will tell of the number of deaths from the virus, in order for you to run out and get the injection, by using fear as a means of coercion. So years down the line, you will see the devastating effects that these injections will do on the masses of the Black race, as in the past. And the government will definitely downplay it, and tell you that it has nothing to do with the vaccinations, which is a lie.

This is a way to eliminate the Black people and the ones that are in poverty, who are already in poor health and lack the proper health care, nutrition, and diet to fight off these experimental diseases made by the government. Take a close look at the amount of poison we have been putting into the air, water, and soil over the centuries. Now you know where the majority of these problems are coming from.

And just the contamination of the earth alone has put people at an elevated risk of poison and disease, so it is impossible to get positive results from fighting poison against poison. These experiments are leading us to self-destruction in the nation and in the world.

These giant pharmaceutical companies have the cure for many of the diseases in the world today, but they will not release the medicine to treat the masses. They are only meant for the wealthy. Instead, they will push all kinds of pills and chemicals on the public, with all types of dangerous side effects, which will do more harm than good. And you have to ask yourself, Why are there so many new diseases in the past fifty years?

So what good is medicine if the prescribed pill that is meant to help you has side effects that are worse than your illness? You will be better off not taking it. Now what do food and drugs have to do with each other, as in the government's Food and Drug Administration? Neither are related, but they are a combined entity. So my take is this: Since the creation of this department, they are telling you right in your face that they are putting drugs in our food, poisoning the people for decades, purposely causing the failed health of millions, and then turn around to continue to poison you with synthetic chemical medicine, with fatal results.

And this is what I call racism, research, experimentation, and elimination of the masses, especially against the Black race. These manufactured chemical drugs are not met to heal you. And some of these deadly drugs that these doctors, prescribe for you to take to treat diseases and illness, they would never take themselves because they know of the devastating consequences of taking them.

Remember, no one knows your body better than you. Yes, a medical doctor can diagnose you and tell you what is happening to your body and the outcome of certain diseases and illnesses, but they can never tell you what or how you are truly feeling. All medicine is not good medicine. Be extremely careful of what you are putting into your body because once you become hooked on their legal drugs, they got you for life. So doctors are nothing more than scientists who will continue to treat the masses, which is why they practice medicine, and we all know the definition of *practice*. So they will continue to practice their experiments on the Black race, for the government, and I refuse to be tricked by these greedy, selfish, diabolical pharmaceutical companies and so-called doctors, who conduct these sick experiments when their only concern is money. This is why the Almighty God is coming to clean up this earth—and soon. It is filled with sin, lies and deceit, and oppression. So it is coming to an end.

CHAPTER 4

Recipe for Racism

Let me try and explain why the problems of today are a direct result of racism of the past when it is continued to this very day. Hate, violence, injustice, and extreme financial suppression—which are the number one issues in this country for Black people—these things have always been used against the Black race of people. It does not take a professor or anyone with a college degree to show the government that racism is going on in America. To expose the truth, all it takes is common sense and close observation of this country's practices and the number of unfair treatments against Black people that are reported on a daily in this unfair country.

So we will examine some of the ingredients, which are in their recipe, as to why there are so many complaints of racism, which are rejected by the White United States government. But I tell you this from experience and facts. Black people do not go around claiming racism just because they are Black. An extremely high number of claims of racism against the Black American population are true and sincere, but these racist White government officials will deny that it is happening today as they have really changed their ways over the past centuries, but it has only gotten worse. Black people have just gotten immune to it over the centuries of oppression. But if you look at the number of books being written about racism in the United States of America, the increased education of the Black race will continue to expose the violent and disrespectful behavior being displayed by racist White America.

Being victims of a society has been against the Black race for centuries. When did it begin? Will it ever end? Will this country ever be at peace when it comes to race relations? This problem should have had some kind of resolution back in the 1960s, but nothing was done to see that equality and reparations were given to the Black race, which is why so many of us are still in poverty to this very day. Yet many foreigners have surpassed us in this country, coming from abroad. From the time I was growing up in the seventies, everything is the same—no change—in any inner-city in the United States, where there is a significant Black population. My grandfather, Royal Cyril Brooks, was a victim of your racist community, in the city of Gretna, in the parish of Jefferson, in the state of Louisiana, in the United States, yet nothing was done about his injustice, and scores of Black people have been tortured, mutilated, disfigured, castrated, murdered, and violated to the point where no one would be held accountable for the crimes committed in this country against the Blacks, yet you want us to forget like nothing ever happened.

So this is the definition of *racism* according to their dictionary: "prejudice, discrimination, or antagonism directed against a person or people, on the basis of their membership, in a particular racial or ethnic group, typically one that is a minority."

But honestly, racism is also used as a means to stop the Black race from gaining financial independence, by owning businesses and real estate, buying and controlling stocks, and owning major banking institutions and manufacturing companies, in order to be self-sustaining people, capable of taking care of themselves in this country.

So this is a fact that the United States government has been using financial racism to keep Black Americans in poverty and dependent upon them. Look at the history of White supremacist government officials destroying Tulsa, Oklahoma, and other Black United States communities during the early parts of the 1900s, that did not require their help. So the killing of Black people and the destruction of their communities were their only alternatives to keep Black people in poverty—they had to obliterate their establishments because they had attained financial independence.

But what has been overlooked is that Tulsa (Greenwood), Oklahoma, was not the original Black Wall Street. Durham, North Carolina, was an advanced, Black Wall Street community before Tulsa. There were also many other Black communities in the northern and southern parts of the United States during the 1900s, including New York and Illinois, which were Black financial hubs that were home to independent, wealthy Blacks in America, who gained financial independence from White America, which White America did not like because the thought process was that these Black people cannot do what we do after getting out of slavery not too long ago. So they destroyed and burned these communities while murdering their Black inhabitants.

Now not only did these White people invent crime in the United States, but they also invented rioting—to keep the Black race from becoming financially independent of the White government— by destroying every Black settlement in the United States with their violent display of hatred.

And to tell you how racist this country is, the only Black establishment in the state of Wisconsin has been totally eliminated from history. Not one building is standing to this very day. It has been razed to the point of nonexistence. There is only a sign that depicts its location. There is not one Black town in that racist White state of Wisconsin, and an overwhelming majority of all of the states in the United States of America!

It is particularly important today that we start to accumulate financial independence and wealth by owning major businesses, which our Black people knew over a century ago. The Black race only owns one-half of 1 percent of anything in this country, but we have over a trillion dollars that we spend on things that we do not own or produce, giving our money back to these White-owned corporations, while our neighborhoods do not receive anything in return. Now if we owned more than just 10 percent of any of these giant manufacturing production companies and corporations in technology, banking, and countless other businesses, look how independent we could become.

Now I ask you this, have you ever seen any other race come into the Black neighborhoods on their payday and shop? So one has to ask the question, why is that?

Our very own people have been brainwashed into thinking that spending your money with other races instead of your own makes you look better in society, which is nonsense because you are able to purchase from the other races when there are many Black companies that offer the same goods and of the same quality, if not better. But our very own people will not patronize our Black-owned businesses, and the few Black-owned businesses need to do a better job by treating Black customers with the utmost respect and thanking them for spending their hard-earned money with their business. So in order for us to remain competitive, we need to start building and maintaining our own hospitals, schools, automotive plants, utility companies, food production plants, police departments—and the list goes on—so that we can employ our own people and become independent from handouts from the government. They will continue to keep the Black race lost and confused, without any type of wealth. We must demand better when voting, and make sure that you hold these Black politicians accountable for being elected officials.

The Black race needs to become united once again and pool our resources together and start wealth building, and instead of living in neighborhoods, we need to seriously start to build communities, businesses, and industries for Black people. Otherwise, the racist White government, will always hold us at the bottom of society and continue to put immigrants of the Caucasian race ahead of us while increasing their population to remain the majority in this country. We have to regain our sense of pride and dignity in a country that continues to keep us oppressed.

Black wealth building is the key to success in America. Otherwise, in the next one hundred years, the Black race will be in the exact same position as today and will be worse off than what the slaves were in during the time of slavery if we are not exterminated by then.

So it is particularly important today for the Black race to start pooling our wealth together and show the United States that we are an exceptional and competitive race of people, and we will not be third-class citizens anymore. We are superior to the White race and second to none or any other race of people on earth. No more grooming us to work on your modern-day plantations. We will not work for you, but we will work for ourselves, and everything that you own, we will own, in order to remain productive in society and keep our money in our groups where it belongs—that is vital to our survival on earth.

We are not going to prepare our people anymore to work for you all of their lives while you pay us a fraction of the wealth accumulated by you that you keep for yourself as you have done for centuries since the beginning of capitalism and by the domination of wealth. The end of your greed begins now.

You have fooled Black people once again, and for too long, with the dream of going to school for a good-paying job, only for them to once again work as modern-day slaves, while the Whites continue to increase their wealth—as you did during the time of slavery—instead of teaching the Black race of how to create their own businesses to be independent, so it is very critical that we start to do it ourselves as of today.

We must start to demand—no more marching and hoping, singing, and wishing. We are demanding because we are the builders of this nation, yet the only thing we and our ancestors have received are broken promises, blood, sweat, tears, lies, injustice, and killings at the hands of the government for many years. And they will continue to use the same old tactics used against the Black race since the beginning of this country. One has to ask the question, how is it that the Black race is in the same position today as when we were slaves yesterday?

White America must be and will be held accountable for the wealth that was stolen from the Black race. How can you deny it? It is impossible, yet you continue to refuse the documented history of your wrongdoings.

This racist society has had a four-hundred-year head start against the Black race, and it will take centuries for us, the Black race, to close the gap in wealth and equality. So will we ever receive justice for the pain and suffering of our ancestors?

From your written law, that you have made, you clearly stated in writing that the Black citizen is a protected race in the United States of America—this is documented, yet you continue to violate our rights to this very day, as citizens and cofounders of this country, even though our ancestors were taken against their will and made to serve you—which is total insanity. The Black race demands justice and the money that the United States of America owes to the true descendants of slavery, point-blank. No more debating, no more stalling; you have to pay what is due, regardless of how much opposition you have from the White people that are against paying reparations.

You know the truth of your insanity and you, White United States of America, have to step up and be accountable. It is time for this country to do what is right—no more debating. We are demanding. The Black descendants of slaves will not wait another year for you to decide whether or not you are going to pay up. How can anyone refuse the truth?

Since the creation of this country, it has been done by design to keep the Black race suppressed and held in a position of subhuman, with no means of equal rights. Every person of the White race is placed above us when they enter this country, which is wrong. That is blatant racism right in our faces. So the question is, how can we become competitive when our rights as human beings are constantly being compromised and being secretly held in modern-day bondage?

But you have to remember that the Almighty God has true documentation of everything that has been done up to the present time, yet you White supremacists continue to suppress the Black race as in the days of slavery. So the saying is true, what happened in the past is repeating itself in the present.

From the many centuries of a planned and calculated plot to try and ban and exterminate the Black race, and the Black foreigners who are oppressed from other nations, from seeking asylum in this country, I will explain to you how the racist White United States of America government continues to use racism and discrimination against the Black people by turning away the Black race of foreign people and will do things to keep the population of the Black race, from increasing on American soil, but in turn, they will justify letting people of the Caucasian race enter into this country—and scores of them illegally—by trying to brainwash the American people that they deserve to come here because of their so-called harsh conditions, but they have a country of their own, where their government should be taking care of their own people.

They have been letting Mexican immigrants and Central Americans walk into the country since the seventies, and they continue to build tunnels into the United States, while breaking federal immigration laws for tens of decades, coming into the United States of America illegally, with no fear of repercussions, and becoming American citizens because many are classified as Caucasian. And they have been doing it for over fifty years, while draining our resources, and in the process, bringing disease and crime into our country. Then you will let Afghanistan's rejects into this country with open arms. You will fly them into this country, at our expense, and then you have the nerve to ask for donations to support these people. And these are the same individuals who are out to destroy the United States of America with their terroristic ways. All because they are classified as Caucasian. Meanwhile, you are increasing the White population dramatically.

Now your bias and racist ways are put on public display for the entire world to see! In the latter part of the month of September 2021, when the immigrants from Haiti, trying to seek a better way of life that many other races have claimed in the United States of America, they are unwelcomed and greeted with hate and resentment. The United States of America resisted with the full force of racism by letting racist White border patrol agents and others of different ethnic backgrounds conduct themselves as though they were overseers, by whipping Haitian immigrants while on horseback, refusing them entrance into the United States! I have never seen a Mexican treated in such a manner, coming into the United States illegally. But look at the way that they treated the Haitian immigrants. Everyone is welcomed here that is White, but the Black Haitians were greeted with such hostile rejection and refusal. And I have never seen the government of the United States, in all of my days as an adult living on earth, move so diligently and swiftly to remove the Black Haitian immigrants away from American soil. They boarded them on aircraft so fast that you would not have known that they were on the border! So I would like to know, why were the Haitians denied the right to seek asylum in the United States of America?

So what is the message that is being sent? They do not want any more Black people coming into America to increase the Black population in this racist-based society. Where are the so-called Black activists, speaking up on behalf of the Black Haitian asylum seekers? Where are the donations for them? Where is the fake concern for their children? Where are the human rights for the Haitians, that other immigrants of the Caucasian race receive when claiming asylum? How come the Haitians cannot be dreamers?

No compassion was given to the Haitians, only hate in this racist-based society. So how should Black Americans feel after entrance into this country was denied to our own race of people?

Where are the so-called Black American leaders at? Somewhere with their tails stuck between their legs, afraid to speak up! They do not care about Black people in this country and in the world because if they speak out, they will be outcasts and lose their butt-sniffing positions and stop eating from their masters' plates. They will also be banned in society because the oath that they have taken prevents them from speaking against the racist White government. How will they help the Black race?

Now you let me know if any of you have seen any immigrant coming illegally into the United States of America being denied entrance, of any race other than the Black Haitians being mistreated the way they were? And it is on film, them being forcefully kept out of this country, since the entire world knows that if you want to get into the United States of America, illegally, all you have to do is come through Mexico and be Caucasian. The Haitians were not placed in holding shelters or processing facilities or granted asylum. They were deported very quickly, and no one spoke up on their behalf. So all you have to do is go through Mexico, if you are an undocumented immigrant, and if your skin is white, they will let any Caucasian in because you look just like them. That is straight racism on display by the United States government and the Mexican government, and they do not care. They have a secret agreement with the United States to continue to populate their own kind, to suppress the Black race—documented facts! And to continue their recipe from centuries ago, they have brainwashed every race, male and female, into thinking that the Black male is a threat not only to their wellbeing and safety, but having them think that we are uncivilized people and all we do is commit senseless crime, which is far from the truth.

So the bottom line is they want a world, without Black people, but the Black race is the cradle of human life, and they resent it with a passion and they hate us. So that is just a portion of some of your diabolical and hateful ways to maintain superiority over the Black race, as you have witnessed for yourself. And they know for a fact that many of the immigrants from Haiti, who were treated inhumanely, have a legitimate federal lawsuit against the United States for violation of their human rights. That is why they got them away from American soil so fast. The American empire is about to crumble, with its two-faced human rights and laws.

The lies being presented for the entire world to see prove just how racist this country is against the Black race, and it shows just how racist they are as they were centuries ago. And they do not plan to change their ways, but only to continue with their elimination of the Black race with what I call their recipe for racism, and there are plenty of ingredients not mentioned.

CHAPTER 5

What Is Fair, USA?

What is really disturbing is that my grandfather, Royal Cyril Brooks, an innocent Black man to whom this book is dedicated, was slain at the hands of a very cowardly, White supremacist, city of Gretna, Louisiana, traffic police officer. He was obviously fearful of an unarmed Black man who did not pose a threat to anyone. But the mindset back then and even today is that we are dangerous criminals; we are liars, robbers, rapists, murderers, and any other despicable category that you could classify us. I have to make this clear: the same goes for every race of people on earth, and I want you to remember that it was a racist White man who murdered my grandfather, and Royal Cyril Brooks is a proud Black man.

To be publicly declared detrimental to society and basically considered a nonfactor in this racist country, to be publicly humiliated and falsely accused of committing crimes when it comes to public opinion—the treatment continues to this very day. Our position in a racist society continues to be magnified, as though we are the reason for the problems of today when we are the victims of being mistreated for centuries and being denied basic human rights because we are Black.

When given the same equal opportunity to better the Black race in this corrupted country, the Black man excels in every aspect of society, whether it is in business, medicine, education, politics, athletics, or any other category. We seem to be superior when given a fair and equal chance, even after centuries of neglect and proven racism in the United States of America. So that would be a start as to why they are in fear of the Black man.

Placing the obvious barricades for centuries up to the present time makes it almost impossible for us to compete in a White supremacist country that will do anything to keep the Black man in a state of chaos and disparity. One good example is how the government, through secret meetings, will inject all types of propaganda into the news media to make it seems as though we are the blame for the many illegal drugs that they have produced. Tell me what pharmaceutical company or laboratory is owned by a Black person living in any inner city in America. It takes millions of dollars to come in contact with thousands of pounds of drugs, legal or illegal. But look at the number of low-level drug peddlers, Black men in particular, being convicted of these drug-dealing offenses, while the major suppliers are rarely being apprehended. And how about the gun violence that is out of control in this country? Everyone in America knows about the quantity of violence being committed on a daily basis, by all races, but how is it that, for some strange reason, Black men are convicted of or are framed for committing felonies? Somehow, they are able to obtain a weapon illegally and are using them against their own people in a manner that is hazardous to their own race. But I do not know of any Black gun or rifle manufacturers in America. So now the main concentration is gun violence, but look at who created the turmoil, when they have been producing deadly and dangerous firearms for centuries. We are blamed once again for something that they have made and placed in society a long time ago when they were the only ones with the privilege of owning and using it.

So, once again, this is just one of their many ways to put the Black man at fault by twisting the narrative so the center of attention is directed at the Black man, and the way the media reports their information makes it seems as though that these things that I have just mentioned, and many more, were created, manufactured, and produced by Black men in the inner city.

So now society has the mindset that we are the inventors of these very terrible things in America, yet this country continues to distribute, en masse, both weapons and drugs, and as the years go by, who is responsible for making the drugs and guns deadlier? And it is not going to slow down anytime soon, and this is when parenting comes into play. I have to make this statement for you to raise your kids properly with faith in the Almighty God and to value all human life and to be aware of the dangers that come with drugs and guns. Nothing good comes out of it.

Now Black America has a moral obligation to start taking care of one another because White America wants us to lose our sense of direction in life. Instead of focusing on *me*, how about focusing on *us*, as a race? It is not that hard. It just takes commitment and dedication for the Black race to become united, because Whites do not care about any Black person, so one would be surprised just how fast things will start to improve, instead of letting someone out of your own race try telling you how to reduce and solve the problems in your community when they are on the outside looking in—they are the ones responsible for your condition today—by supplying you with misinformation, lies, and deceit to hold you back as long as possible until they can get rid of you.

Now with that being said, society has inserted in the minds of all races that all Black men commit crimes, which is false. But when we encounter another person of a different race or sex, we are watched very closely, including the Black women. Now I will give you an incredibly good example of what I have recently experienced. I was inside of my parked vehicle, waiting for my wife to come out of the supermarket, and this Black lady, who was parked two cars away from me, saw me sitting in my car. She immediately started watching me, afraid to pull off, as though I would follow her. I ignored her; not once did I look her way, and I'm definitely not thinking about her. I glanced to see who was walking at the back of my vehicle. She was visibly paranoid, so she honked her horn and flashed her lights while in her car. So my question is this, why would you think that just because a Black man—minding his own business while sitting in his Lincoln navigator, not looking at you at all—would be planning to do harm to you while you are inside the safety of your car when you could have gone about your normal business? See what I mean?

I couldn't believe her reaction to seeing a Black man sitting in his SUV. And another example really takes the cake. While at the post office at 9:00 a.m., I was sitting in my Lincoln town car. My wife had just gone into the post office to pick up a package, so while she was in the post office, an old elderly Black lady happened to come out. I understand that women have to be aware of their surroundings—and I tell my wife and two adult daughters to be aware too—but check this out. She immediately stared me down. Not once did I look at her; I saw her in the corner of my eye. She stared at me from the time she walked out of the post office until she had gotten safely into her car, but instead of going about her business, she watched me for over ten minutes, thinking that I would follow her, I guess. So why wouldn't she just pull off, while in the safety of her vehicle? I am not thinking about her. So she stayed park, being afraid to move. She thought that I was thinking about her, so she continued to watch me, which I thought was strange, until my wife came out of the post office. Then she stared at my wife, who had an exceptionally large package, and this idiot still would not pull out of the parking lot until me and my wife pulled out to go about our business. And she had the nerve to pull in back of us. I couldn't believe her demeanor— she was that shook up. And on top of that, I hate to say, neither of them was attractive. They were mutts, one old and one middle-aged, afraid of a Black man. And I drive an up-to-date Lincoln navigator and a Lincoln town car, so I know I don't look suspicious, or at least I hope not.

So as you can read, this is the type of attitude that they have labeled upon the Black man. Also, why would you even think that anyone would want to bring harm to you? So the mindset is when you see a Black man, you think that we are criminals, and you automatically think that we are thinking of doing harm to you, which is total nonsense.

Also, why would you be worried about anyone that is not paying any attention to you, or even looking your way? And I am quite sure that if a criminal wanted to do a crime, they would not let you get into your vehicle safely, doesn't that make sense? So my take is this, you do not need to be out in public if you think that every

Black man you see sitting in their car in a public parking lot would commit a criminal act, while dozens of people are going back and forth to their cars. I do not think criminals work that way. But you are watching a respectable Black man while he is minding his own business. How stupid can you be?

Now another way of starting a conflict with a Black man is this: When interacting with White people and other races of non-Black people, they try and use disrespectful and racist remarks to see what kind of reaction they can get out of you, which I experience on a daily basis when dealing with non-Black individuals. And the one thing is when you use their disrespectful comment and direct it right back at them, they become upset, then that is when they will become irritated and try to start conflict or an argument to make it seem as though you are starting a commotion. Their subtle approach is to disrespect you with sly and condescending comments that are meant to degrade and belittle you, and that is when you have to correct them about the word usage that they are directing toward you because they think that you do not know the meaning of the insult which is being hurled at you. So you have to stay alert to what they are saying very closely because they—meaning Caucasians and other non-Black races—will insult you every chance that they can.

And it is so sad that many Black people do not understand the disrespectful language being used until it is explained by someone who does know. Do not tolerate this type of behavior being displayed by White America or any other non-Black race—it is racism. As I told you earlier in my book, you have to pay attention to word usage and phrases because they are taught that the majority of Black people are illiterate.

Now we move on to housing in the United States of America. Since the time of slavery, Black Americans have always been neglected and given hand-me-downs from slave masters, until today. And this is what I mean: Once the Whites began their mass exodus from the cities across America and moved to their newest development called the suburb, who do you think received their used, raggedy homes? Black people did. However, the Whites enjoyed the privilege of brand-new homes, modern technologies, up-to-date electrical advances, asbestos-free and lead-free plumbing and paint, and many more upgrades to homes that were newly built. This is what the Black people received and are currently getting today: used homes, decades old, that are filled with an abundance of deadly and hazardous material, including lead-based water pipes and paint, along with homes insulated with toxic asbestos that's known to cause cancer, especially if the home is not properly renovated. Not to mention these homes are also vermin-infested with all types of diseases. That is what was given to just about every inner-city Black resident in the United States of America as of today.

Worn-down structures, many of which are a century old, and in many cases, over one hundred years old, on the Eastern seaboard located in the United States of America. These dwellings should have been razed fifty years ago, if not sooner. Now these homes are breeding grounds for all of the illnesses that these Black residents are being exposed to since the 1960s.

But the United States of America government will not make a commitment to have these homes destroyed nationwide. It is like nothing is going on with these dilapidated and hazardous dwellings. These homes are dangerous to the health and wellbeing of our Black children, and the government knows it. Why do you think so many of our Black children, have elevated levels of lead poisoning and all types of medical and learning disorders? They would rather have us thinking that saving the animals or saving a dog or a cat instead of saving the Black men, women, and children is more important! They will treat any animal, wild or domestic, better than a Black human being.

Go to any inner city in the United States, where there is a Black population, and look at what they call home. It is a shame, but we have no other place else to go. Now you see why we were given secondhand housing across this country, and no one seems to bring up this discussion to the attention of the government. I wonder why. Is that fair? Is that equal? Is that because we are the descendants of slaves and because we are meant to be inferior in this racist society? Or is it when the Declaration of Independence was written, the Black race of people were not included and shall always be equal to a field animal, three-fifths of a human being, not equal to a White person?

And that's racism big time, but no one cares about the condition that the Black race is in. These homes will kill you. Here is a good analogy. Poorly insulated homes, where you will freeze in the winter, because of badly worn, outdated windows and doors; leaking roofs; inefficient heating; and disease-carrying pests, and you will sweat and be miserable during the summer, with lack of air conditioning, causing your utility bills to soar out of control because you run a fan all summer, which is designed to keep you in debt by these White-owned utility companies. This is what millions call home, but nothing is being addressed about this racism, and they want you to spend thousands of dollars for something like what I just described to keep you struggling all of your life.

Black America, do not continue to be treated in this manner as modern-day slaves. If you are in the market for a new home, make sure that you receive a new home, where you are the first inhabitants. Do not settle for used; we've been given hand-me-downs for centuries. Refuse what has been used by others. Now is the time for us to receive brand-new everything, especially when it comes to current homeownership.

So we have to realize as of today, why and how we are being mistreated in society, and the answer to that is you were never classified as a human being, since the beginning of the founding of this racist country. You will never be equal to Whites because they have you distracted with your main concern of getting a new car or trying to get money and living like the racist White supremacists of this country. But in reality, you'll never catch up to them or live as lavishly as them because it is their solemn duty to keep you in the crab barrel and as poor as you can be. It is documented written law. Do your research, Black America. The results will shock you, but it is true facts!

So the only thing the Black race can do is to continuously demand that the United States of America do the right and fair thing and pay the reparations that are owed to the Black race in this country, not mixed-race Black people or foreign Black people who do not have a right to reparations in the United States but DNA-assessed true descendants of slaves whose ancestors were held in bondage and exposed to the inhumane treatment, which did not end not too long ago while we are still feeling the effects of slavery to this very day. All you have to do is look at the condition that our Black people are in, all across this country, compared to our White counterparts and other races of immigrants.

Is that fair? But they will say that we have made progress, all the while you are dwindling our population down through all types of a planned and calculated process of elimination from the world. This country will never come clean and admit to the crimes that have been done and continue to do to the Black race after centuries of slavery. The government cannot continue to use racism against the Black race and expect us not to rebel. We are in a new millennium; this must come to an end.

Instead of talking about and laughing at the condition that the Black race is currently in, particularly, the Black man, we should be trying to solve this problem of injustice directed solely at the Black race. We have been marching and hoping for an exceedingly long time, and frankly, we should be tired of doing that for change to happen, and the only thing that we receive are lies along with broken promises, while the main focus of the government is to eliminate the Black race and to create more ridiculous laws so that they can finish incarcerating the Black man. And if they can get you tricked into committing a foolish, senseless act of violating any of their written laws, once you are caught up in the system and out of society, inside of any of these barbaric, sick, and dangerous penal facilities, you might as well be declared dead, because that's h——on earth. Then you will know exactly, what it is like being a slave.

Not only do they know the devastating psychological effect that being locked up has on the human mind, but that is one way of breaking down the human's morality, both physically and mentally damaged, no matter who you are. And if you do happen to be one of the lucky ones to make it out alive, you are damaged for the rest of your life because of the horrors that you have witnessed that go on in these modern-day plantations. Also, just because someone can trick the system into thinking that they are rehabilitated, you run the risk of them committing or repeating the same act that sent them into the prison system in the first place. So how can that help anyone trying to re-enter society, when being sent to a place that is supposed to correct you, but instead is designed to kill you or make a person more hateful and dangerous from being incarcerated?

No matter what an individual says, they are never the same once you spend time in any of these human zoos. They have issues that they will take to their grave, and the sad part about it is that these so-called psychologists will tell you they are fine, normal enough to re-enter society.

So once again, America, what is fair? And to make this truly clear, there is an abundance of many more problems going on in this dysfunctional society that you have made.

CHAPTER 6

Mis(sed)information

Mis(sed)information is a customary practice of what the government of the United States has always given to the Black race to keep us in a state of confusion. Now the news that is received by Americans through different media outlets, has drastically changed over the past century. With the invention of the radio, television, internet, social media, and cell phones, news travels at an incredible speed from coast to coast. True events unfold across the nation. News information is captured on cell phones, good and bad. Once there are images recorded—a photo is taken or a recording has been made—there is no denying what occurred or what took place. Cell phone cameras are everywhere. Now in 1948, there were not any cell phones. We had to rely on the camera and human witnesses, but they are just as effective and dependable as a cell phone photograph in having documented images and facts of an event. So I ask this question: Why was not the picture of Royal Cyril Brooks—my grandfather who was murdered in broad daylight in the middle of a United States of America street, at the ferry landing bus stop in Gretna, Louisiana, on February 27, 1948, at 3:00 p.m., in front of many witnesses, over the dispute of a five-cent bus fare by a cowardly, racist White traffic police officer from Gretna, Louisiana—used as evidence against that racist police officer? No weapon was found on Royal Cyril Brooks, nor was a weapon found near his body, only he was slain, clutching a bag of peanuts.

This police officer was acquitted of first-degree murder, which is what I call mis(sed)information. How can you disregard eyewitnesses' statements and a picture proving that Royal Cyril Brooks was murdered by a racist White police officer? And the sad thing about it is that there were White witnesses captured in the photo from 1948. So how is that photo different from any other photos taken today, except for the one taken in 1948, in black and white?

Now in order to confuse the racist White public into thinking that the police officer conducted himself in a professional manner according to the law enforcement protocol, the mass media outlets twisted the information by injecting all types of false narratives about the event that occurred which resulted in the murder of Royal Cyril Brooks, and by presenting these lies to the racist White citizens of Jefferson parish, city of Gretna, Louisiana. Just about every White citizen in that locale assumed that my grandfather had broken the law, and it wouldn't have mattered if he was accused of stealing a one-cent piece of bubble gum, it would only have taken for him to have broken any of their written laws for the murder to have been justified in a racist community. But he helped a White lady out because she boarded the wrong bus, and the bus driver refused to refund her five-cent bus fare. That's when my grandfather intervened, only trying to possibly help solve the argument ensuing between the White female bus passenger and a very arrogant, disrespectful, and unprofessional White bus driver so that my grandfather would avoid being late for work—not committing any crime whatsoever, but the only thing that Royal Cyril Brooks received from being a respectable and honest citizen, was a felony assault, and an unjustified killing, at the hands of a racist, White, sick, so-called law enforcement officer. And I hold the bus driver accountable for playing a role in the death of my grandfather by lying and saying that he had broken the law by refusing to pay a second fare after my granddad had given his fare to the White lady so that she could board the correct bus since the bus routes have been changed without any notice given. So why could he not ride on her paid fare when she did not object to it? That practice has been done thousands of times before, so why would this time, be any different?

So by placing doubt and lies into the minds of an already extremely racist, southern White community about what really happened, it swayed an already White supremacist community in the deep south that, whatever took place, the crooked police officer was honest, even though he was a racist murderer. That is why he was protected even though murder has been committed. So how could my grandfather receive a fair trial if he is deceased and Black witnesses are threatened with violence and death if they testify, putting their families at the risk of being murdered by the KKK? And retaliation is very real in Louisiana.

And yes, I am speaking facts because all of the information that I have received, I have gotten from my aunt Bertha Mike (Brooks), my father's oldest sister, who I lived with in Marrero, Louisiana. She is also the oldest daughter of Royal Cyril Brooks. And I also had the privilege to meet my grandfather's second wife, my step-grandmother, Mary, who my grandfather wedded in holy matrimony after the death of my father's (Herman L. Brooks) mother. Herman's mother died after my dad was born. And to make it perfectly clear, my uncle, Roy Brooks Jr., happened to make it to my grandfather at the Gretna, Louisiana ferry landing bus stop in 1948 before he passed away after being shot down by this racist, disturbed, cowardly, and unprofessional so-called police officer—who did not deserve to be on the police force, which clearly shows that he has no respect nor regard for Black human life. My uncle is in the photo from 1948. He is sitting on the curb—not believing what has happened to his father—after his dad was brutally and violently murdered at the hands of a racist White police officer for no logical reason or explanation; committed by a police officer employed by the city of Gretna, Louisiana Police department. And these things have been happening all over, regardless of what year it happened, in the United States against the Black race, with no one held accountable because it was okay in the eyes of racist White America.

So what I am trying to articulate is that the truth and facts and information from the murder of Royal Cyril Brooks in 1948 have been changed and concealed. Concerning the death of my grandfather, his story has been purposely manipulated and the facts have been distorted and information hidden so that the outcome of his murder is justified, according to the unfair and racist White law enforcement in Gretna, Louisiana, and Louisiana's crooked judicial system, which made it where a Black man, in the eyes of racist White public opinion and a racist White government, thoughts of what is right, instead of justice being served in a so-called blind-to-race-or-skin-color justice system, in a racist-based society. So if you are a Black person living in America during the Jim Crow era, which is semi-slavery, you will not receive any justice. The only thing you will get is a swift kick in the rear end or death, case closed.

So if you read the facts and documentation of the case which has been researched and proven to be an unjust murder of Royal Cyril Brooks, how could any professional district attorney or public representative in a court of law, including the judge, call being unarmed and shot in the back and in the side at point-blank range, justifiable? What would have happened if a Black police officer had shot a White man in the back in 1948? God only knows. The only way an individual can do that is if they are racist and they clearly hate Black people and had not the faintest knowledge that civil rights change was occurring right before their eyes for Black citizens in America.

So no one can tell me if that was not mis(sed)information, and mis(sed)information done on purpose, done by a racist White system that controls the information given to the public and the corrupted city of Gretna, Louisiana, police department, who refuses to publicly admit it, in one of the most racist states in the United States of America.

See, one of the main reasons why my grandfather was murdered, from a Black man's point of view, is that they, meaning the White supremacists, resented the fact that Royal Cyril Brooks, being a respectable, kind, and intelligent Black man, did not let skin color interfere with him helping out a White woman who was clearly having a challenging time with someone of her own race.

And my grandfather helping that White woman out resulted in him being slaughtered in broad daylight. And nothing would be done about the injustice done to Royal Cyril Brooks, and nothing would be mentioned about the racial injustice until seventy years later. So the Jefferson parish government was hoping that the story would not be discovered by the descendants of Royal Cyril Brooks, so what kind of justice is that? But here I am, writing about this atrocity that happened to my grandfather over seventy years ago, and I will not let that racist town forget as long as I live what was done. See, you know about the three grandchildren who were born in Jefferson parish that are Royal Cyril Brooks' grandchildren—and God bless my cousin, Tyrone Brooks, who recently passed. We were close, and he was like a big brother to me—but what you did not know is that my oldest brother, Cyril D. Brooks, who is the oldest grandson of Royal Cyril Brooks, was born at Charity Hospital in New Orleans, Louisiana, and my grandfather has a total of eight grandchildren by his son, Herman L. Brooks, and the eight children's mother, is Joan E. (Williams) Brooks of Marrero, Louisiana. For anyone who likes to try and question the validity of my true but tragic story, this is real facts and information.

So I will never let the city of Gretna, Louisiana, police department forget about the racist injustice and the violent and inhumane murder of my grandfather, and neither will any of my siblings—and my grandfather have plenty of great-grandchildren and great, great-grandchildren, who will continue to pass his story down, to the next generations to come. This life-altering event will haunt this racist, sick community to the end of time. And I will make certain that my grandchildren will remember the story that I am writing about to pass it down to their children. And if you want to know, I have two granddaughters and one grandson.

So the Brooks legacy will be continued from the west bank area across from New Orleans through me, by writing two books about my grandfather's unlawful death, regarding him being murdered of his life in racist White America, and by the hands of the blue racist law enforcement organization. And what is very misleading is where do they find these sellout types of Black news reporters from? Because they are recruited to report the news against their own race with mis(sed)information, and they have to report it, according to how the White racists see it.

Now another way to get mis(sed)information is to control all aspects of the media by using manipulation, racism, and propaganda to influence the thinking of White Americans. The domination of mass media, which the three major outlets are television, radio, and major newspapers in the country, enables them to get their point of view—and no one else's—across the nation. They are run by racist White supremacists by having total control of the information industry. They own over 1,200 newspaper companies in the country compared to the slightly over one hundred newspaper companies which are owned by Black people. They have superior control of 393 local television stations throughout the nation, compared to only ten owned by Black people throughout America. And finally, they have control of over 15,000 radio stations while Black people only own a mere 168. Remember that the numbers may fluctuate. So after being on this soil for an exceptionally long time, who do think is getting their message across and controlling the information which is being told to the nation? Mis(sed)information is currently showing that we cannot get our opinion across in this racist society. And by having that kind of power, they are able to control public opinion or the truth spoken pertaining to the events happening in America through our eyes, but what they say goes, so it is impossible to receive true reporting of the news. Why do you think when you read, listen, and watch the news, Black people seem to make up the majority of the negative headlines being reported to the masses, yet we make up only 12.4 percent of the population? But we are the main topic of discussion, every single day and night, across the country. I understand the need for information in the nation, concerning everyday life, but the mis(sed)information that is being put out to the masses is making life extremely difficult for Black people to get a fair and equal chance at life in America when there is racist reporting done, especially when we are constantly under the microscope. So they will continue with their bias and damaging mis(sed)information and will never let us tell the story of what's going on in this country or where we live. We can only work for them, and we have to commentate what they write. If we are employed by them, and if you go against their directive, you will be without a job, and good luck if you are trying to get hired in that profession after being banned in that occupation. Black people are not only being denied ownership of mass media but we are also being rejected. Look at the treatment of constantly, and purposely, being censored of ownership of anything major in mass media.

Keeping the doors deliberately shut and not receiving any type of opportunities to get involved in the information industry is the continued use of racism, and we are not even aware of how they blatantly stop us from owning and producing anything pertaining to resources or information so we have to rely solely on the Caucasian race for our information and products. So how can you believe anything that is being reported by them when their main objective is to keep you in a submissive state of mind? And can you think that everything being reported by them is honest, fair, and truthful when they have a history of lies and deceit?

So once again, their continued domination of every aspect of life here on earth, in all categories, the media will always be under their control until the equal distribution of economic resources and information are available to the Black people, which the White supremacists will refuse to spread equally. They will protest adamantly because they will not want to share anything with the Black race, and nothing can be done about it, no matter how much, the Black race tries to resist racism because it has been written in code to keep the Black race equal to a field animal, and they have sworn with their souls to the dark side to always keep the Black race in an inferior position as long as they control this country and the world.

And just in case there are those who do not believe, there is research to prove everything that has been written in this book as I continue this explanation of blatant racism, wrongful killings, and the tricks used by White supremacists, along with their diabolical RREE, and their recipe and mis(sed)information. Nothing is fair about America when it comes to addressing the problems of Black citizens in the United States. White America and the racist White world will never give in to fairness, equality, and the distribution of wealth and resources when their only concern in this world is to maintain superiority, domination, and control over the Black race and every other single race of nonwhite people on earth, and to keep control of all of the destructive and life-eliminating weapons that they have made on the planet. And there is nothing anyone or any race can do about it. It is a fact of life, and it is what is going on in the world today.

And to let everyone know that I will make it noticeably clear that you may think that there are going to be changes to how law enforcement conducts itself in the future, but you better believe that there will not be any changes made. The Black politicians and so-called Black political activists that claim that they speak on behalf of the Black citizens in America, who have sworn in secrecy never to speak of what they will do for the Black race or to speak publicly of what the Black citizens need in order to survive and remain competitive in this country or say it in public, they will be outcasted and removed out of their position. It's a strong possibility that they will be set up to face criminal prosecution or slander and be ruined of their credibility to the point of no repairing in the Black public eye. And to make it perfectly clear, not one so-called Black politician or Black political activist speaks up on my behalf. I speak for myself!

So I say this to Black America, you better start to pay close attention to what is going on in this country, and how the government system is being run because everything is repeating itself for Black Americans. All you have to do is take a keen look around you and how your people are living and the condition that they are in.

CHAPTER 7

Judicial System, Failed

This is a failed and very corrupted and poorly investigated murder in the United States by law enforcement, as usual in America during the Jim Crow era, when it concerns a Black man who was accused of breaking the law. This so-called investigation was conducted by the city of Gretna police department in the state of Louisiana. It was performed by an extremely racist judicial system. It was a very inefficient investigation, regarding the murder of Royal Cyril Brooks, a Black man, in Gretna, Louisiana, in 1948, so how can his death be reported as a justifiable homicide when he was clearly shot in his back, unarmed, and not committing a crime? How did the judicial system fail Royal Cyril Brooks?

How were you able to make it seem as though a crime was committed by influencing the jury to find the police officer innocent? How did the district attorney not see that a first-degree homicide was committed by a law enforcement officer, and the district attorney was supposed to have a degree in law? Why was this incompetent police officer protected from prosecution?

How was the law enforcement department and the judicial system in 1948 able to persuade a racist, all-White, all-male jury that the police officer was innocent of murdering an unarmed Black man when the Black man did not break the law? Why weren't the witnesses' truthful observations by the people of Jefferson parish of what really occurred taken seriously or used in a court of law?

And finally, how did the jury find a police officer who shot an unarmed man in the back innocent, when he was guilty of committing a homicide? I can continue this closing chapter with many questions, but I will not. I have to dig a little deeper into this flawed investigation. The answer to the above questions is that racism and White supremacy played a significant role which would determine the outcome of the trial.

There was not anything that could have been done and nothing that could have been said to make a racist jury or community believe otherwise, and no one would be able to refute their decision of justice.

There was a handful of so-called prominent Black government representatives at that time in the United States, but none that I know of would denounce the unjustifiable and senseless and cold-blooded murder. My realistic thought is that if they would have spoken up about the tragic incident done to my grandfather, they would have been killed or kicked out of office. So Royal Cyril Brooks, a Black man, would not receive justice in a country as racist as America. The proof is in the documented history of their wrongdoings. But hundreds, if not thousands, of wrongful deaths that have been done to Black Americans by law enforcement go untold in history.

When I read about the facts that occurred in 1948 leading up to the death of my grandfather, his skin color, injustice, and racism against him played an extremely significant role in determining whether or not my grandfather would receive a fair and equal trial against the White supremacist law enforcement community in Gretna, Louisiana, even though he was slain over seventy years ago in a very racist town.

No matter how hard you try, you cannot convince me that this racist investigation, done by the blue organization, was not an obvious cover-up, designed to protect a White supremacist police officer who had committed several felonies against Royal Cyril Brooks. So how could Black Americans receive fair and equal accountability of the law during the Jim Crow era, when we are treated less than human? What about the letter that was sent to then-president Harry S. Truman or the inquiries made to United States Attorney General Tom Clark, who both were in office in 1948? They ignored the letter and pleas sent on behalf of Royal Cyril Brooks, and there was no statement given or consideration to the Black life that was unjustly murdered. They closed their eyes and refused to hear the truth, unwilling to acknowledge the brutal, unprovoked killing done by a White police officer when they know for a fact that it was wrong and the law was broken. Now when a White person is killed or there is an unjust murder committed against a Caucasian person, there is an uproar in the community, and all available resources and police force are used at their disposal—at the expense of the taxpayers—to find out whoever is responsible for the crime that has been committed. And please, do not let a Black man be accused of the killing, because if he happened to have killed a White person, in 1948, he was as good as dead, whether he is innocent or guilty. And before the White mob takes his life, he will die a slow death because he will be tortured and would be subjected to a very cruel and sadistic death. In the meantime, a very professional and diligent investigation is done for the White person. They will go over everything with a fine-toothed comb because they will leave no stone unturned, and every witness is interviewed and every piece of evidence will be checked, even if it takes them years, to get the murder solved. But when it comes to a Black person, it will be poorly investigated, steps missed, information not reported, documents lost or misplaced, or just an outright dereliction of duty because a Black person has been killed and they just do not care to properly perform their job because it pertains to a Black person being murdered.

So the fact of the matter is that Black people do not receive justice when a crime has been committed against us, only injustice, which continues to this very day, and nothing has changed since the beginning of this racist country when Black people have been mistreated, dragged in the dirt, murdered, and overlooked as a human being by White supremacists running this country.

So as you read, when a White law enforcement officer, anywhere in the United States, has killed a Black person unjustly, they are protected by the government judicial system at all costs because they have been placed on a pedestal by the title that they have been given by the government, and they are classified as a superior type of human who speaks the truth honestly 99.9 % of the time, and different from the rest of the citizens, which is one of the biggest lies told to the country. They are granted immunity if they can, somehow, make the killing justifiable in the eyes of the public. These police officers, who act out these grisly types of deeds against the Black race, are able to go home to their families as though nothing has been done and knowing that they have beaten the system, but the victims of the crime that have been wronged will have a lifetime of mourning and no hope for receiving justice in a racist judicial system, run by White supremacists.

So how is it that Black people receive a different type of justice compared to White people when Whites are a protected class in America? When you read or hear of a police-officer-involved shooting or killing, almost always, it involves a Black man being murdered at the hands of White law enforcement, and not just recent beatings and killings, but a history of violently beating down or killing Black men whenever they feel like it. And it has been done for centuries. So how do we expect them to stop doing something that has been embedded in their genealogy? Because hate and resentment are a reality in this country, and it has been directed toward the Black race through the tactics used by the government and performed by law enforcement agencies all over the country. This type of behavior will continue, as told by the White officials, and it seems as though only the Black man is being exterminated from this planet and no other race of man is receiving what we are getting through legalized killings. And nothing is being done to combat this form of genocide.

So two of the main culprits against the Black man are this racist judicial system and the law enforcement. By voting in these corrupted judges, both Black and White, along with these women judges who are Black male haters, they claim to be fair, but how can you be neutral when you are locking up Black men on a daily basis all year long? Now do you realize it is not very many of us left in this country who are free because the majority of us are incarcerated? We know of the obvious criminals that commit crimes, but you have to take a close look at the disparity in the sentencing of the Black man. Taking away their freedom just because you are a so-called judge, while you are having the public believe that you are more trustworthy than another person on earth. You are fallible; you are not the Almighty God, but you demand respect from anyone that enters your unjust courtroom.

You better come back to reality and have your house clean because your time is limited on earth, like everyone else, and when your time is up being a caretaker on this planet, like the rest of us, make sure your life is in order—since you think that you are living without sin—because you are about to meet a real judge, the Almighty God.

And I hope that you can remember all of the Black men that you have sentenced unjustly and whose life you had turned into a living nightmare by sending them to prison, taking away their life because you thought that they were guilty when they had sworn to God that they were innocent of the crime that you said that they have committed, but look at all of the killer police officers across the nation that you have believed to be innocent of murder, that you have set free because of a title given to them by the government. And you have set them free because they were White and they are a protected race in this country, yet they were guilty of killing a Black man because they felt like it and they knew that they would be protected by you, a so-called judge, with the help of a racist district attorney lawyer, who is just like everyone else, yet all of you walk around here like you are better than anybody who does not work for your racist judicial system or law enforcement. I will never kiss any of your butts, and I do not have any respect for you, and I am not afraid of any of you, not one judge in America, after how my grandfather was murdered by the hands of law enforcement. So, what are you going to do about the injustice?

Now what we really have to figure out is what is the purpose of having four court systems and this country, when breaking the law, according to their definition is a crime? And all of them should be treated in the same manner, right? And should be held in the same courtroom, so why do they have four classifications of court systems—city, state, and federal, with the most powerful, being the supreme court in America? It is confusing because they say it is the type of crime, which has been committed. But think about it. Crime is crime, but the way the system is structured determines the type of justice which will be handed out or received. Is it one for Whites and one for Black people, one for superior humans (the rich) and one for the inferior human beings (the poor)? Because from the looks of things, it seems as though the Black race always gets the short end of the stick.

Now we all know that these low-level judges are voted in by corruption in order to maintain control of the Black race by using female judges to make it seem as though we are getting fair accountability of the law, but take a look at how the supreme court judges get into office. They are appointed, which we all know, and these so-called supreme court justices are given a lifetime position until they die, and they have taken a sworn oath to keep the Black people from receiving fair and equal accountability of the law in America, just like the only Black supreme court justice, whose job is to keep his own people in the crab barrel.

So how is that fair and equal toward the Black race? And after being on this American soil for centuries, you would have thought that Black Americans would have had more than one token Black on the supreme court, because the rest of them are extreme White racists, which is why they were appointed, and that way, you cannot vote them out. And if you take an incredibly good look at the one so-called Black supreme court justice, he is not a Black man; he is one of these sell-out Black people who think that he is White. And with the fact that he is a so-called Black man, they put him in place to suppress his own people. He does not do anything for Black people in this country. Everyone knows his name; I do not have to remind the masses because he is a clown and a very cowardly individual and he is extremely afraid of the White man.

And not only that, but I also have to say that out of all of this racist, discriminatory women's movement that is going on in this country—which the White man is behind to destroy every Black successful male figure—explain to me why, did they not put this so-called Black supreme court justice, on blast, who was accused of sexual harassment against one of their very own so-called precious Black woman? Why wasn't he put on the chopping block, like all of the others? Since they like going back in the past, which they have done to many other Black men, pulling up accusations from years ago, of our Black role models and celebrities?

The reason they did not mention his past as they have done to so many others, is that he is protected by the White racists, and one of the main characters who is protecting him is our current president. He protected him from prosecution back in the 1980s, with the help of thirteen other racist White government officials, of the exact same laws that he has sworn to uphold when he was appointed to the highest court in the land, but he was accused of breaking the law himself. So as long as he is doing his job by keeping his own race suppressed and not speaking up for them, as far as equal treatment goes, he will continue to stab his own people in the back, sell us out, and look the other way when it comes to fairness and equality for the Black race. He does not care for the Black people and that bougie individual that they have appointed to the supreme court of the United States of America—which is supposed to be a symbol of justice for the Black race—hates Black people with a passion and that is what we have to deal with until he dies, and that is a hard pill to swallow for the Black race.

So once again, how can you call the judicial system is fair? Because if you are an average Black man, living in the United States, and you are accused of breaking the very same law, would twelve White men come to my rescue? I doubt it very seriously. If anything, they will be trying their best at throwing me beneath the jail, unless I am one of their protected pets that has served them loyally in keeping my own Black people suppressed.

So the structure of the judicial system, from the beginning of this country, was specifically intended to keep the Black race of people from gaining equality and justice in a racist society, and it is going to be an uphill battle with these racists in getting them to change these very racist laws that have been written from centuries ago. This is the type of behavior that's been conducted against the Black race, so we'll be singing and wishing, hoping, and crying for the next two hundred years unless we start to demand change today—not tomorrow—concerning all aspects of life in a country who will stick to their plan with blatant racism right in our Black people's faces, along with a calculated plot of elimination from the planet, so we must wake up, Black America. Otherwise, our future is in jeopardy.

Thank you for reading my book. I hope that you enjoyed it, and may the ALMIGHTY GOD bless you.

This is a quote that I have written: "Disappointment is nothing new, nor is it a surprise to a Black man in the United States."

Royal Cyril Brooks (1903–1948)

This is the author and the grandson of Royal Cyril Brooks.

www.ingramcontent.com/pod-product-compliance
Lightning Source LLC
Chambersburg PA
CBHW031000180726
47993CB00018B/1183